Are You Sure?

Learning about Proof

A Book of Ideas for Teachers of Upper Secondary School Students

Introduction

The need to be sure that mathematical results are true makes the idea of proof vital to the activity of the mathematician. It is right therefore, as an important aspect of the school mathematics curriculum, to focus on proof, with its accompanying need to understand and be able to generate chains of logical reasoning. Concerns have been expressed that this important aspect of the subject has been relatively neglected in the school curriculum in recent years. As a consequence, many students entering higher education have not developed either a sufficient appreciation of the importance of proof or the skills of understanding proofs and of generating their own proofs. However, the idea of proof has an important place in the mathematical education of all students. We hope that the book will make a small contribution to making proof more accessible and enlightening to a greater number of those who study mathematics.

The book has been written to discuss some of the issues related to learning about proof and to provide a source of ideas for teachers to use in the classroom. The level of the material is for the most part appropriate to students in the final three or four years of secondary education and includes ideas of varying levels of difficulty. The book has been designed to be dipped into: individual chapters and sections within chapters are largely independent of each other. Questions and exercises are provided throughout, with detailed commentaries in the final section of the book. In addition to providing ideas for teachers the book also provides a valuable resource to which abler students can refer, both to extend their understanding and appreciation of particular topics and to broaden their mathematical education. Permission is given by the Mathematical Association for purchasers to photocopy relevant sections of the book for use in their institutions.

Acknowledgements

This book about proof has been produced by the AS and A level sub-committee of the Teaching Committee of the Mathematical Association, and has been edited by Doug French and Charlie Stripp.

The members of the sub-committee, who have contributed to the book, are:

Barbara Cullingworth	Jenny Orton
Stephen Drape	Charlie Stripp
David Forster	Sally Taverner
Doug French	Peter Thomas
Christine Lawley	Marion Want

The members of the sub-committee would particularly like to record their thanks to Keith Barnett, Jan Jagger, Mike Price, Melissa Rodd, Mark Thornber and to many others who have helped in various ways in preparing the book for publication.

Using this Book

This book does not provide a comprehensive review of proofs from the whole school mathematics curriculum, but rather highlights a number of topics by presenting some less well known results and proofs, and by comparing different proofs of the same result. The book need not be read sequentially: individual sections within each chapter may be read independently.

Key results and statements are highlighted in boxes edged with a single line, whilst boxes edged with a double line and headed 'Try This' contain activities designed to consolidate or extend some of the ideas of the section. Possible solutions, and some discussion for each of the activities, are given in the commentary at the end of the book. Shaded boxes contain brief biographical notes on some of the mathematicians mentioned in the text.

Reading about mathematics is not like reading a novel. A novel is normally read straight through without any need to pause and think, or to re-read part in order to clarify some point. Some suggestions are given here about the sort of strategies which are helpful when reading mathematics and, in particular, when trying to make sense of a mathematical proof.

- Always skim-read a proof first, to get a general idea of the form the argument takes.

- Identify the key ideas involved, and do not be distracted initially by details which are not central to the main purpose.

- Be prepared to be persistent – some parts may need to be read several times to make sense of them.

- Constantly ask yourself questions about what you are reading.

- Have pencil, paper and calculator available and use them to check calculations, fill in missing details, try out special cases, draw diagrams and clarify arguments.

- Aim to understand thoroughly – identify any words and symbols whose meaning is not clear.

- Think carefully about the logic of the arguments.

- If something fails to make sense after several attempts, read on – it may fall into place when the argument has been developed further.

- Discuss it with somebody else. Trying to reason things through together can often be very helpful.

- Chapters and sections of chapters in this book, and many other books, are not necessarily arranged in order of difficulty, so do not be discouraged too readily by difficulties at an early stage.

- If something does not make sense today, try again tomorrow – starting afresh often results in you looking at previous problems from a different perspective.

Examples of proof by contradiction are on pages 35, 41 and 48, of proof by induction on pages 35, 41 and 51 to 57, and of proof by exhaustion on pages 12 to 15.

Contents

Chapter One

Why Proof?

Is It True?

$$\boxed{0.\dot{9} = 1}$$

Is it true that $0.\dot{9}$ is equal to 1? To many people it seems obvious that $0.\dot{9}$ is a bit less than 1, and, therefore, the two are not equal. It is often very difficult to convince them that their intuition is wrong. The purpose of a mathematical proof is to establish without doubt that something is true by presenting a reasoned argument. So, here are four ways of looking at this particular result for you to think about. Further discussion about them will be found in the commentary at the end of the book.

1. A numerical argument

   If $0.\dot{9}$ is not equal to 1, then either it is less than or greater than 1. Usually it is thought to be less than 1. However, if it is less, then there must be a number which lies between $0.\dot{9}$ and 1. If you cannot find such a number then this suggests that they are the same.

2. Continuing the pattern

   If $\frac{1}{9} = 0.\dot{1}$, then $\frac{2}{9} = 0.\dot{2}$, $\frac{3}{9} = 0.\dot{3}$, ... and so on to $\frac{9}{9} = 0.\dot{9}$. Therefore $0.\dot{9} = 1$.

3. An algebraic argument

   Let $n = 0.\dot{9}$, so that $10n = 9.\dot{9}$.

   Then $10n - n = 9.\dot{9} - 0.\dot{9}$, so $9n = 9$ and $n = 1$.

4. Summing a geometric series

   $0.\dot{9} = 0.9 + 0.09 + 0.009 + ...$, which is an infinite geometric series with first term $a = 0.9$, and common ratio $r = 0.1$.

$$\frac{a}{1-r} = \frac{0.9}{1-0.1} = 1.$$

Proof is an important part of mathematics because it is necessary to establish whether results are true and can therefore be trusted both as tools for problem solving and as building blocks for further ideas. Common sense and intuition cannot always be trusted: what seems to be obvious may on careful examination turn out to be wrong or, at least, more complicated than it at first appeared. Likewise, arguments like those given above may look very plausible at first sight, but they also need to be viewed critically to detect any faulty reasoning or hidden false assumptions.

Wanting to know why things are true, rather than passively accepting results and formulae, is an important part of developing an enquiring mind, and is an essential attitude when learning mathematics. Making sense of proofs requires a background of appropriate knowledge and skills, together with an ability to think clearly and critically.

What is Proof?

The notion of mathematical proof can be difficult for learners because the word is used with different meanings in everyday conversation, in the media and, particularly, in science and mathematics lessons. In common with many other words, such as *similar* and *difference*, it has a distinct meaning when used in a mathematical context. Scientists, who may be considered to be our academic cousins, use the word *proof* in a distinctly different way than mathematicians. Before we consider what mathematical proof is, it may therefore be worth considering what mathematical proof is not!

> A mathematical proof is not reasoning from empirical evidence.

A scientist makes observations and sets up experiments which generate results to provide empirical evidence to test a particular hypothesis. If a large amount of such evidence supports the hypothesis, and nothing is found to contradict it, then the hypothesis is considered to have been 'proved'. The hypothesis is then referred to as a theory, but there is always the possibility that new evidence may be found which may cause the theory to be modified or even rejected. Scientific evidence is usually based on measurements which must inevitably be approximate – however great the degree of accuracy, they can never be exact. In many respects scientific proof is similar to proof in a court case where guilt has to be established 'beyond reasonable doubt' using the evidence that is available.

For a mathematician, evidence may suggest that a particular conjecture is true, but that is not sufficient to prove the case. Drawing five hundred triangles, and then measuring and finding the sum of their interior angles, does not prove that the angle sum of a triangle is 180 degrees. A mathematical proof requires a reasoned argument from previously established results, or from a set of axioms which are statements accepted as truths. When a *conjecture* in mathematics has been proved it is called a *theorem*, whereas in science, a *hypothesis* that has become widely accepted is referred to as a *theory*. However, both in mathematics and science, the word *theory* is used, in a quite different sense, to refer to a body of deduced results such as *the theory of numbers*.

> A mathematical proof is a reasoned argument from accepted truths.

If a mathematical proof is wrong it is either because there is an error in the reasoning, or because there is an error in the underlying assumptions. A scientific proof may have errors for either of these two reasons, but it may also be wrong because it does not take account of some piece of contradictory evidence whose existence may not even be suspected at the time, or because results could not be measured with sufficient accuracy.

Unfortunately, some widely-used mathematics coursework tasks do tend to encourage the scientific idea of proof by suggesting that it is sufficient to test a conjecture for a few specific cases. This can lead to confusion in the minds of students about the idea of a mathematical proof. A mathematical proof, whilst it can take many different forms, must provide a reasoned argument why a given result holds for all situations. It is not sufficient to show that it works for a few, or even a large number, of specific cases, unless all the possible cases can be considered. If there are only a finite number of cases (or a finite number of types of case), then a proof by exhaustion may be appropriate, but commonly there are an infinite number of cases and a different approach is needed.

Types of Proof

It is often easier to prove that a false conjecture is false than it is to prove that a true result is true. A proof may require a complicated and lengthy chain of reasoning, but a single *counterexample* is all that is needed to show that a conjecture is not true. However, counterexamples, even when they exist, are not always easy to find, so that, for some results, it is often far from obvious whether they are true or false.

There are many mathematical statements which have yet to be disproved or proved. One of these is Goldbach's Conjecture. In a letter to Euler in 1742, Christian Goldbach (1690-1764) wrote that every even number greater than two is the sum of two primes. It is possible to show that this is true for all even numbers up to a million, and beyond, but, as you should now be aware, such evidence is far from being a proof that it is true for all even numbers. Perhaps you could be the one to produce either a counterexample or a proof of Goldbach's Conjecture!

Five different types of mathematical proof (or disproof!) are considered in this book:

- *Disproof by counterexample*, where, as discussed above, a single example is sufficient to show that a conjecture is false. A famous example is Fermat's conjecture that all numbers of the form $2^{2^n} + 1$ are prime, which is true for values of n from 0 to 4, but is not true for $n = 5$. It took a mathematician of the stature of Euler to find this counterexample by showing that 641 is a factor of $2^{32} + 1$.

- *Proof by deduction*, where a chain of deductive steps leads from some accepted truths to the new result. A simple example is to prove that the sum of a natural number and its square is always even. Since $n^2 + n = n(n+1)$, you see that the sum is a product of two consecutive numbers and then deduce that it is even, since one of a pair of consecutive numbers is even. Most proofs in this book are deductive, but deduction also plays an essential part in all types of mathematical proof.

- *Proof by exhaustion*, where all possible cases are systematically considered. The example of the sum of a number and its square can be proved by exhaustion by considering the two possible cases of odd numbers and even numbers. This conveniently reduces the infinite number of cases to just two. With an odd number the square is odd and the sum of two odd numbers is even. Similarly, for an even number, the square is even and the sum of two even numbers is even. The important element in such a proof is being systematic in ensuring that all possible cases have been considered – not always as simple as just two cases of odd and even. Further examples of proofs by exhaustion are to be found on pages 12 to 15 in Chapter 2.

- *Proof by contradiction*, where assuming the opposite of what was to be proved leads to a contradiction. Assuming that the sum of a number and its square is odd immediately leads to the contradiction that a number and its square are of opposite parity (one odd and one even). Further examples of proofs by contradiction are given on pages 35 and 41 in Chapter 3 and page 48 in Chapter 4.

- *Proof by induction*, which is most commonly used for results that are true for all the natural numbers. The aim usually is to show that the truth of the result for one value implies truth for the next value. Then, if the result is true for some particular starting value, it is true for all subsequent values. Proofs by induction are discussed at length on pages 51 to 57 in Chapter 4.

Each type of proof has its own particular logical structure which must be understood if a proof is to make sense. In a proof that involves a lengthy argument or a great deal of symbolic manipulation it can be easy to lose this overall structure and fail to see the wood for the trees.

Mathematical conjectures and theorems are statements of the form 'if P then Q' or 'P implies Q', which can be expressed symbolically using the *implication* sign as $P \Rightarrow Q$. Here are two examples of such statements:

$$n \text{ is odd} \Rightarrow n^2 \text{ is odd}.$$

$$n \text{ is positive} \Rightarrow n^2 \text{ is positive}.$$

Both statements are similar in form and both are true, but they differ in one important respect which becomes clear when the *converse* of each statement is considered:

$$n^2 \text{ is odd} \Rightarrow n \text{ is odd}.$$

$$n^2 \text{ is positive} \Rightarrow n \text{ is positive}.$$

Here the first statement is true, but the second is false because the square could be the square of a negative number. It is important to realise, as this simple example shows, that the converse of a theorem is not necessarily true. In the 'odd' case the implication holds in both directions and the statements are *equivalent*, as denoted by a double-headed arrow:

$$n \text{ is odd} \Leftrightarrow n^2 \text{ is odd}.$$

Another way of speaking of implication is to use the language of *necessary* and *sufficient* conditions. For n to be positive it is a *necessary* condition that n^2 is positive, but it is not a *sufficient* condition because n could be negative. Further examples where converses are discussed will be found on pages 36, 37 and 40.

Whatever the type of proof, it may involve one or more of the following different approaches:

- Proof using words. A proof does not have to have any symbolic statements – a simple sentence or two may suffice. For example, to prove that the product of any three consecutive numbers is a multiple of 6, you only need to note that any set of 3 consecutive numbers must include both an even number and a multiple of 3.

- Proof using pictorial representation. Many geometrical proofs are conveyed, in essence, by a picture. The diagram proving Pythagoras' Theorem on the front cover of this book (and discussed on page 18) is a good example.

- Proof using algebraic reasoning. Many proofs do inevitably involve more or less extensive chains of algebraic reasoning, because algebra is such a powerful tool for expressing generality and developing arguments in a succinct abbreviated form.

The book contains a wide range of examples of each type of proof with a variety of different approaches. Of course, it is not always possible to put specific proofs into one distinct category, because they may involve elements of more than one. In many cases different proofs have been given for the same result, because an alternative approach often gives fresh insight.

Learning about Proof

The Cockcroft Report noted that *'mathematics is a difficult subject to teach and learn'*, and proof is often considered to be a particularly difficult aspect of mathematics. Mathematics without proof provides a very limited view of what the subject is and greatly restricts the stimulation and interest that it can provide. We would therefore challenge many of the prejudices that are held about proof and its potential place in the school curriculum by putting forward a number of statements for debate.

> Proofs are accessible to more than a gifted few.

Many proofs are very short and simple to follow: this book includes a range of examples of varying levels of difficulty in each chapter, so that there is plenty that will make sense to a wide range of learners.

Proof is not something that is just for the older and abler student. An intelligent young child can produce a simple proof by contradiction to prove that there is no largest number, by noting that you can always find a bigger number than any number that you suppose to be the biggest, by simply adding 1. Many students in the early years at secondary school can readily appreciate a proof that the angle sum of a triangle is 180 degrees based on the properties of parallel lines.

Obviously some proofs will be longer and more demanding, and there are many proofs that are beyond the scope of this book (and its authors)! For example, the proof, recently produced by Andrew Wiles, of Fermat's Last Theorem has taken over 300 years to establish and can be fully understood only by a few mathematicians. The proof is immensely complicated and very long, drawing on a wide range of mathematical areas, and yet the theorem itself is very simple to state, namely that, for any integer $n > 2$, there are no positive integer values of x, y and z which satisfy the equation $x^n + y^n = z^n$. Simon Singh's book *Fermat's Last Theorem* gives a popular account of the search for the proof.

> ## FERMAT (1601-1665)
>
> Pierre de Fermat was born in Toulouse and became a lawyer. He is best known for his work in number theory. He claimed in a marginal note to have found a proof for his last theorem, but he never published his proof. Given the subsequent difficulty that the search for a proof has caused, it must remain doubtful whether his claim was true.

> Proofs do not always require lengthy algebraic arguments.

Mathematics is a language with its own specific and distinct meanings for words and symbols. We have tried to avoid just using algebraic arguments, although they obviously do play an important part in the presentation of many proofs, and in other aspects of mathematics. However, a proof does not have to involve lengthy algebraic reasoning: a sentence or two, or a picture, may be sufficient to convey the essential truth. At the end of some proofs you may indeed ask yourself *'Is that it?'*!

Proofs are not just a product of the past.

The history and development of mathematics is long and complex and many cultures have made significant contributions to our mathematical understanding. However, mathematics continues to grow and develop, and new proofs, both of well established and of recently discovered results, continue to be produced today. This is particularly so with the increased processing power of computers and the growing knowledge base on which the subject can draw. Indeed, as this book was being written, a new generalisation of Fermat's Last Theorem, known as Beal's Conjecture, has been publicised. It states that, for any 3 integer exponents m, n and r, all greater than 2, there are no positive integer values of x, y and z which satisfy the equation $x^m + y^n = z^r$. No counterexample has yet been found using extensive computer searches, so the conjecture is still awaiting either proof or refutation.

Proofs are 'on the syllabus'.

The ability to reason in a logical manner, drawing on a range of established results, is a skill well worth developing for its own sake, not simply because of any specific syllabus requirements. However, there is an expectation of an understanding and appreciation of mathematical proof in the school curriculum, both in the National Curriculum for England and Wales (1995), in the A level core (1999), in their Scottish equivalents and in the International Baccalaureate.

The mathematics National Curriculum for England and Wales (1995) only mentions the word 'proof' once when itemising the further material in Key Stage 4 for Attainment Target 1 'Using and Applying Mathematics'. It states that :

Pupils should be taught to extend their mathematical reasoning into understanding and using more rigorous argument, leading to notions of proof.

The 1999 A level core specifies, in section 3.3.1, three items which relate to proof, of which only a) and b) are required for AS level.

a) *Construction and presentation of rigorous mathematical arguments through appropriate use of precise statements and logical deduction.*

b) *Correct understanding and use of mathematical language and grammar in respect of terms such as 'equals', 'identically equals', 'therefore', 'because', 'implies', 'is implied by', 'necessary', 'sufficient' and notation such as $\Rightarrow, \Leftarrow$ and $\Leftrightarrow$.*

c) *Methods of proof, including proof by contradiction and disproof by counter-example.*

The core also refers to proof in one of the five assessment objectives. Assessment objective two (AO2) states:

Candidates should construct rigorous mathematical arguments and proofs through appropriate use of precise statements, logical deduction and inference and by the manipulation of mathematical expressions, including the construction of extended arguments for handling substantial problems in unstructured form.

Chapter Two

Geometry and Trigonometry

The Angles of a Triangle

You are familiar with the fact that the angles of a triangle add up to 180°. A quick and easy way to demonstrate this for a particular triangle is to cut off each of the corners and rearrange them in a straight line.

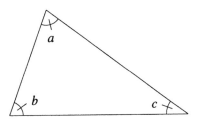 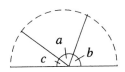

$$a + b + c = 180°.$$

Is this adequate as a proof? There are two major difficulties with it.

- The demonstration involves one particular triangle. How do we know that the same thing applies to all triangles?

- We are relying on the judgement of our eyes. The angles could add up to 179° or 181° – how can we be sure it is precisely 180°?

If the demonstration above seems convincing then look at this apparent proof by cutting and rearranging.

2.1 Try This

Cut up an 8 by 8 square and rearrange the pieces to make a 5 by 13 rectangle as shown. What is the area of each figure?

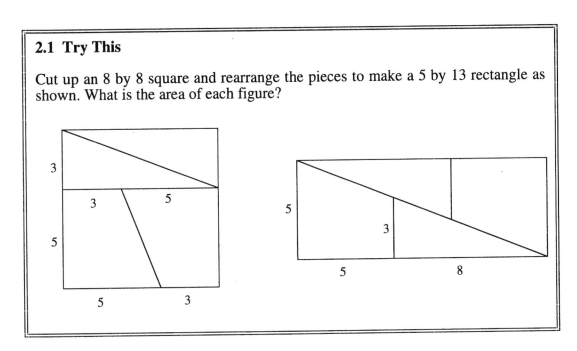

As an exercise in drawing and measuring, you may have been asked to verify the angle sum result. The same thing can be done more dynamically using a geometry package such as Cabri Géomètre or Geometer's Sketchpad. This involves:

- Drawing a triangle and measuring the angles.

- Adding the angles.

- Moving the triangle to see that the angle sum remains constant.

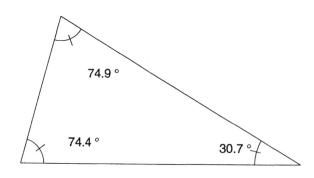

$$74.4° + 30.7° + 74.9° = 180°.$$

Computer packages can, however, give misleading results. They are very useful for looking at a range of examples and enabling conjectures to be made, but proof involves some form of mathematical argument that shows that a result is always true. Verification that something works in a few cases is insufficient, however plausible it may look.

For example, if we use graph plotting software or a graphical calculator to draw the graphs of $y = x$ and $y = \sin x$, with x in radians and the ranges $-0.1 \le x \le 0.1$ and $-0.1 \le y \le 0.1$, the two graphs look identical, but this is clearly not so with ranges of $-1 \le x \le 1$ and $-1 \le y \le 1$. Adjusting the range may give other cases where they still look identical, but it is obviously not difficult to set the ranges to show that the graphs are actually very different! It is usually easier to show that a false result is false than it is to show that a true result is true.

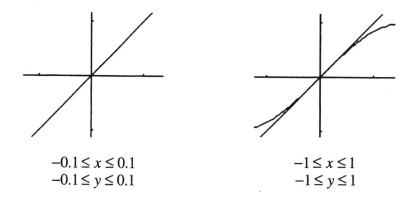

| $-0.1 \le x \le 0.1$ | $-1 \le x \le 1$ |
| $-0.1 \le y \le 0.1$ | $-1 \le y \le 1$ |

Attempts to show that something is true by looking at particular cases can never be successful when there are an infinite number of possibilities – you cannot look at every triangle! You need a proper mathematical proof, which involves a clear argument based on established facts. So, here are two formal proofs of this simple, but fundamental fact about triangles.

> The sum of the angles of any triangle is 180°.

Proof 1

First consider right-angled triangles.

A rectangle has four right angles. Splitting any rectangle along a diagonal produces two congruent right-angled triangles. Why are they congruent?

Any right-angled triangle can be represented as half a suitable rectangle.

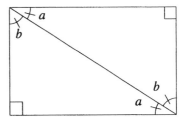

Adding up the angles:

$$(a+b+90)+(a+b+90) = 4 \times 90$$
$$\Rightarrow \quad a+b+90 = 180.$$

So the angles of a right-angled triangle add up to 180°.

Now consider any triangle.

Any triangle can be split up into two right-angled triangles as shown, although it may be necessary to rotate the triangle to obtain a suitable base.

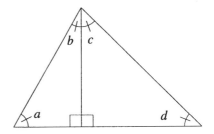

Using the result for right-angled triangles, we then have:

$$a+b+90 = 180 \quad \text{and} \quad c+d+90 = 180.$$

Combining these gives:

$$a+(b+c)+d = 180.$$

It follows that the angles of any triangle add up to 180°.

Proof 2

The corner-cutting method discussed at the beginning of this section uses the fact that the angles of the triangle can be arranged to sit on a straight line. This suggests the method of proof which is to be found in Euclid's *Elements*.

Consider triangle ABC. The line BC is produced (extended) and the line CD is constructed so that it is parallel to BA.

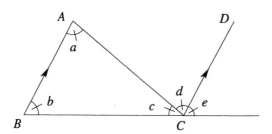

Using angle properties of parallel lines, it then follows that:

$$d = a \qquad \textit{alternate angles}$$
$$e = b \qquad \textit{corresponding angles}$$
$$c + d + e = 180 \qquad \textit{angles on a straight line.}$$

Hence, $a + b + c = 180$ and so the angles of a triangle add up to $180°$.

2.2 Try This

Use the diagram below to suggest a variation on this proof.

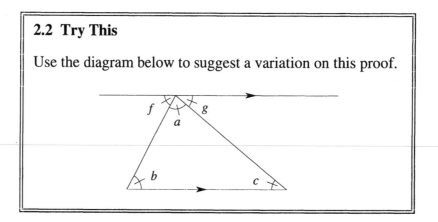

EUCLID

Euclid was a Greek mathematician who is thought to have lived in Alexandria in Egypt in the third century BC. Little is known about the man, but his name lives on as the author of the best-selling mathematics textbook of all time – the *Elements*, a treatise which brought together all the geometrical knowledge of the time in a logical sequence of theorems and proofs. The book continued in use as a school textbook until the early years of this century and has been a major influence in setting the pattern for rigorous mathematical argument for over two thousand years.

The Angles of a Polygon

Here are three different ways of using the angle sum of a triangle to show that the sum of the angles of a convex polygon is $(n-2)180°$ (or one of the equivalent forms $(2n-4)$ right angles or $(n-2)\pi$ radians). A convex polygon is one where all the interior angles are less than $180°$, so that all the vertices point outwards.

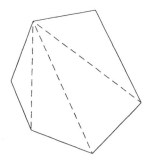

Joining one vertex to each of the other vertices gives $(n-2)$ triangles, and each triangle has an angle sum of $180°$. Hence, the angle sum of the polygon is:

$$(n-2)180°$$

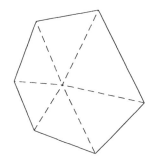

Joining an interior point to each of the vertices gives n triangles. So the sum of their angles, less the $360°$ at the interior point, is:

$$180n° - 360° = (n-2)180°$$

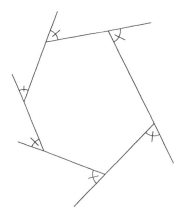

Walking round a polygon and considering the total angle through which you turn, shows that the sum of the exterior angles of a polygon is $360°$. Drawing polygons using LOGO further emphasises this key property.

At each vertex the sum of the interior and exterior angles is $180°$ and there are n vertices. So the sum of the interior angles is again $360°$ less than $180n°$.

$$180n° - 360° = (n-2)180°$$

A variation on the third example is to note that, for a regular polygon, the exterior angle is $\dfrac{360°}{n}$ and so the interior angle is $180° - \dfrac{360°}{n}$ (or these could be taken as the mean values for the exterior and interior angles of a general polygon). The angle sum is then:

$$n(180° - \frac{360°}{n}) = 180n° - 360° = (n-2)180°.$$

The Five Platonic Solids

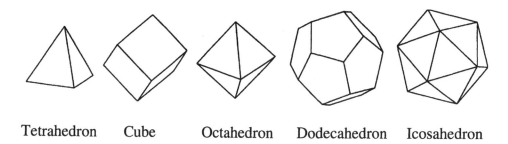

Tetrahedron   Cube   Octahedron   Dodecahedron   Icosahedron

A polyhedron is described as *regular* when all its faces are congruent regular polygons and all its vertices, considered as the edges meeting at each point, are congruent. It has been known since ancient times that there are just five regular polyhedra, as shown above, and these are usually named after Plato. A proof of this appears as Proposition 18 in Book XIII of Euclid's *Elements*, the last proposition in that lengthy treatise and a fitting culmination to the success of the mathematics of ancient Greece.

> ## PLATO
>
> Plato was a Greek philosopher and mathematician who lived in the fourth century BC. He linked the regular polyhedra to the four elements earth, air, fire and water from which the Greeks considered all matter was made in an early form of atomic theory. He reserved the dodecahedron for the shape of the whole universe in his theory.

To make plausible in a simple way that there are just five regular polyhedra, consider the regular polygons that can form the faces and how they can be arranged. This is best seen by working with some cardboard polygons. Indeed, it is worthwhile making models of the complete set of Platonic solids.

- 3 equilateral triangles at each vertex gives a *tetrahedron*.

- 4 equilateral triangles at each vertex gives an *octahedron*.

- 5 equilateral triangles at each vertex gives an *icosahedron*.

   6 or more equilateral triangles at each vertex is not possible. *(Why not?)*

- 3 squares at each vertex gives a *cube* (or *hexahedron*).

   4 or more squares at each vertex is not possible.

- 3 regular pentagons at each vertex gives a *dodecahedron*.

   4 or more regular pentagons at each vertex is not possible.

   Regular polygons with 6 or more sides cannot be used. *(Why not?)*

You may be convinced by this argument, although you may suspect that there could be some more – possibly using lots of triangles arranged in some ingenious fashion. An alternative argument uses the same type of *proof by exhaustion*, but approaches the problem algebraically. This proof makes use of Euler's Formula.

$V - E + F = 2$, where V is the number of vertices, E the number of edges and F the number of faces for any simple polyhedron.

It is worth just verifying that the result does hold for the five regular solids:

Tetrahedron	$V = 4,\quad E = 6,\quad F = 4$
Cube	$V = 8,\quad E = 12,\quad F = 6$
Octahedron	$V = 6,\quad E = 12,\quad F = 8$
Dodecahedron	$V = 20,\quad E = 30,\quad F = 12$
Icosahedron	$V = 12,\quad E = 30,\quad F = 20$

Here is a simple argument which makes Euler's Formula seem plausible:

You can imagine a polyhedron blown up like a balloon to make a sphere with a network of lines on it. This will retain the same values for V, E and F.

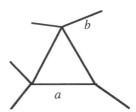

Part of such a network is shown in the diagram. You can remove edges (or arcs) one by one in two different ways. Removing an edge like a on the boundary of a face reduces both E and F by one, but leaves $V - E + F$ unchanged, since $V - (E - 1) + (F - 1) = V - E + F$. Removing a free edge like b reduces both E and V by one, but leaves $V - E + F$ unchanged, as before. Eventually you are left with a single vertex, no edges and a single face (the whole surface of the sphere). Then $V - E + F = 2$, since $V = 1, E = 0, F = 1$. From this, it appears that $V - E + F$ must always take the same value 2 for any polyhedron.

A completely satisfactory formulation and proof of Euler's Formula is beyond the scope of this book. A wide-ranging discussion of some of the difficulties can be found in the book *Proofs and Refutations* by Imre Lakatos.

EULER (1707-1783)

Leonhard Euler was born in Switzerland and spent most of his life working at the St. Petersburg Academy in Russia. He was a prolific mathematician who made a wide range of contributions to the subject. The letter e used as the base of natural logarithms is said to be taken from the initial letter of his name. In connection with networks he produced a famous paper which proved the impossibility of a solution to the problem of the seven bridges of Königsberg.

Here is a proof, using Euler's Formula, that there are precisely five regular polyhedra. It is an example of a *proof by exhaustion*, where all the possible cases are considered systematically. It does, however, assume the *existence* of the polyhedra – plausible pictures or models are not sufficient to show this, but the necessary calculations to show that each is possible will not be considered here.

Consider a regular polyhedron whose faces are regular polygons with n sides.

Then, $nF = 2E$, because, when you count the edges of all the faces, each edge is counted twice, as each edge is shared by two faces.

Let r be the number of edges at each vertex.

Then, $rV = 2E$, because when you count the edges at all the vertices you count each edge twice, as each edge is connected to two vertices, one at each end.

Substituting for V and F in $V - E + F = 2$ gives:

$$\frac{2E}{r} - E + \frac{2E}{n} = 2.$$

Dividing by $2E$ and rearranging then gives:

$$\frac{1}{n} + \frac{1}{r} = \frac{1}{E} + \frac{1}{2}.$$

Since a polygon must have at least three sides, and at least three edges must meet at each vertex of a polyhedron, we have to find values of $n \geq 3$ and $r \geq 3$ which satisfy the equation above.

$n = 3, r = 3 \quad \frac{1}{3} + \frac{1}{3} = \frac{2}{3} \; \Rightarrow \; \frac{1}{E} + \frac{1}{2} = \frac{2}{3} \; \Rightarrow \; \frac{1}{E} = \frac{1}{6} \; \Rightarrow \; E = 6 \; \rightarrow \;$ a *tetrahedron*.

$n = 3, r = 4 \quad \frac{1}{3} + \frac{1}{4} = \frac{7}{12} \; \Rightarrow \; \frac{1}{E} = \frac{1}{12} \; \Rightarrow \; E = 12 \; \rightarrow \;$ an *octahedron*.

$n = 3, r = 5 \quad \frac{1}{3} + \frac{1}{5} = \frac{8}{15} \; \Rightarrow \; \frac{1}{E} = \frac{1}{30} \; \Rightarrow \; E = 30 \; \rightarrow \;$ an *icosahedron*.

$n = 3, r = 6 \quad \frac{1}{3} + \frac{1}{6} = \frac{1}{2} \; \Rightarrow \; r \geq 6$ is not possible, since $\frac{1}{E} + \frac{1}{2} \leq \frac{1}{2}$ for $r \geq 6$ and this would imply a negative (or infinite) value for E.

$n = 4, r = 3 \quad \frac{1}{4} + \frac{1}{3} = \frac{7}{12} \; \Rightarrow \; \frac{1}{E} = \frac{1}{12} \; \Rightarrow \; E = 12 \; \rightarrow \;$ a *cube*.

$n = 4, r = 4 \quad \frac{1}{4} + \frac{1}{4} = \frac{1}{2} \; \Rightarrow \; r \geq 4$ is not possible.

$n = 5, r = 3 \quad \frac{1}{5} + \frac{1}{3} = \frac{8}{15} \; \Rightarrow \; \frac{1}{E} = \frac{1}{30} \; \Rightarrow \; E = 30 \; \rightarrow \;$ a *dodecahedron*.

$n = 5, r = 4 \quad \frac{1}{5} + \frac{1}{4} = \frac{9}{20} \; \Rightarrow \; r \geq 4$ is not possible.

$n = 6, r = 3 \quad \frac{1}{6} + \frac{1}{3} = \frac{1}{2} \; \Rightarrow \; n \geq 6$ is not possible.

You will see that the individual cases follow the same pattern as considered previously when fitting regular polygons together, but we should now feel sure that nothing has been omitted.

Three Polygons at a Point

There are only six sets of three regular polygons (all different) such that the three polygons are coplanar and fit together exactly at a point.

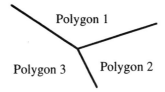

Polygon 1

Polygon 3   Polygon 2

If the three polygons are to fit together, the three interior angles at the point must add up to $360°$. The interior angle of a regular n-sided polygon is $\dfrac{180(n-2)}{n}$ degrees. If the number of sides of the three polygons are a, b and c, all different, then:

$$\frac{180(a-2)}{a} + \frac{180(b-2)}{b} + \frac{180(c-2)}{c} = 360.$$

On dividing by 180 and simplifying this becomes:

$$1 - \tfrac{2}{a} + 1 - \tfrac{2}{b} + 1 - \tfrac{2}{c} = 2 \quad \Rightarrow \quad \tfrac{2}{a} + \tfrac{2}{b} + \tfrac{2}{c} = 1 \quad \Rightarrow \quad \tfrac{1}{a} + \tfrac{1}{b} + \tfrac{1}{c} = \tfrac{1}{2}.$$

Now you need to find sets of positive integers (a,b,c) that fit this relationship. Suppose that $a < b < c$. Since a triangle has the least number of sides, a must be at least 3 and, since $3 \times \tfrac{1}{6} = \tfrac{1}{2}$, a must be less than 6. So the only possible values for a are 3, 4 and 5. Consider these three cases.

When $a = 3$: $\quad \tfrac{1}{b} + \tfrac{1}{c} = \tfrac{1}{2} - \tfrac{1}{3} = \tfrac{1}{6}$.

In this case the only possible values for b are 7, 8, 9, 10 and 11, which give the values for c as follows:

$$b = 7 \;\Rightarrow\; c = 42. \qquad b = 8 \;\Rightarrow\; c = 24. \qquad b = 9 \;\Rightarrow\; c = 18.$$

$$b = 10 \;\Rightarrow\; c = 15. \qquad b = 11 \;\Rightarrow\; \text{no solution}.$$

When $a = 4$: $\quad \tfrac{1}{b} + \tfrac{1}{c} = \tfrac{1}{2} - \tfrac{1}{4} = \tfrac{1}{4}$.

The only possible values for b are 5, 6 and 7, which give the values for c:

$$b = 5 \;\Rightarrow\; c = 20. \qquad b = 6 \;\Rightarrow\; c = 12. \qquad b = 7 \;\Rightarrow\; \text{no solution}.$$

When $a = 5$: $\quad \tfrac{1}{b} + \tfrac{1}{c} = \tfrac{1}{2} - \tfrac{1}{5} = \tfrac{3}{10}$.

The only possible value for b is 6, but this gives no solution.

Therefore the only possible sets of values for (a,b,c) are:

$$(3, 7, 42) \quad (3, 8, 24) \quad (3, 9, 18) \quad (3, 10, 15) \quad (4, 5, 20) \quad (4, 6, 12)$$

Area of a Trapezium

The formula for the area of a trapezium is $\frac{1}{2}(a+b)h$, where a and b are the parallel sides and h is the height. This section presents four proofs of this result. As with most proofs in geometry, a diagram underlies the main idea in each case.

1. The trapezium is made into a rectangle.

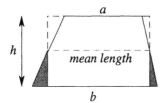

The mean length is $\frac{1}{2}(a+b)$.

The shaded pieces are rotated by 180° as shown.

So, the area is $\frac{1}{2}(a+b)h$.

2. Two congruent trapezia are placed to make a parallelogram.

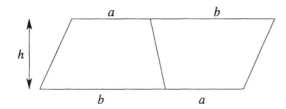

The area of the parallelogram is $(a+b)h$.

So, the area of the trapezium is $\frac{1}{2}(a+b)h$.

3. The trapezium is divided up into a triangle and a parallelogram.

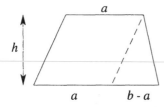

The area of the parallelogram is ah.

The area of the triangle is $\frac{1}{2}(b-a)h$.

So, the area of the trapezium is
$$ah + \tfrac{1}{2}(b-a)h = \tfrac{1}{2}(a+b)h.$$

4. The trapezium is split into a rectangle and two right angled triangles.

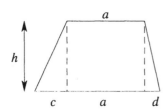

From the diagram, $c + a + d = b$.

$$\begin{aligned}
\text{Total area} &= \tfrac{1}{2}ch + ah + \tfrac{1}{2}dh \\
&= \tfrac{1}{2}h(c + a + d + a) \\
&= \tfrac{1}{2}(a+b)h.
\end{aligned}$$

Pythagoras' Theorem

For a right-angled triangle, the square on the hypotenuse equals the sum of the squares on the other two sides.

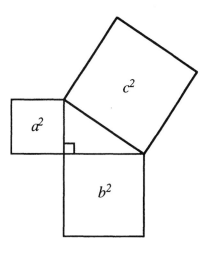

$$a^2 + b^2 = c^2.$$

Pythagoras' Theorem is one of the most famous theorems in mathematics. Although it is commonly named after Pythagoras, it was known well before his time both in China and, at least in some particular forms, to the Babylonians.

PYTHAGORAS

Pythagoras came from the Greek island of Samos and lived in the sixth century BC. Little is known of the man, but he is thought to have founded a group known as the Pythagoreans, whose ideas were part mystical and part mathematical, extending to number as well as geometry and the famous theorem which bears his name. Triangular numbers and the golden section are examples of familiar ideas that interested the Pythagoreans.

2.3 Try This

Eight different proofs of Pythagoras' Theorem are given in the pages that follow.

In each case the picture is an important part of the proof.

Try constructing each proof for yourself by just looking at the diagram.

Proof 1

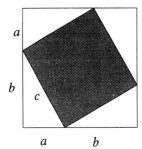 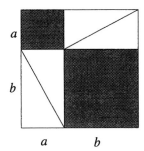

The diagram immediately suggests that $a^2 + b^2 = c^2$, by considering the equal areas of the squares. The right-hand diagram can be obtained from the left-hand one by translating the top right triangle to a position adjacent to the one at the bottom left. The other two triangles can then be translated to form the rectangle in the top right corner.

Alternatively, a more formal proof can be based on the left hand diagram:

Each triangle has area $\frac{1}{2}ab$. The total area of the four triangles is $4 \times \frac{1}{2}ab = 2ab$.

The large square has area $(a+b)^2$.

Then, from the left hand diagram: $(a+b)^2 = c^2 + 2ab$.

Multiplying out and simplifying gives $a^2 + b^2 = c^2$.

Proof 2

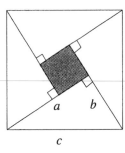

In this diagram four congruent right-angled triangles are arranged inside a square with each hypotenuse, of length c, lying on one of the sides. The sides of the small square in the middle are of length $a - b$, where a and b are the lengths of the other two sides of the triangles.

Since the area of the large square is equal to that of the small square together with the four triangles:

$$(a - b)^2 + 2ab = c^2.$$

On multiplying out and simplifying, Pythagoras' Theorem follows:

$$a^2 + b^2 = c^2.$$

Proof 3

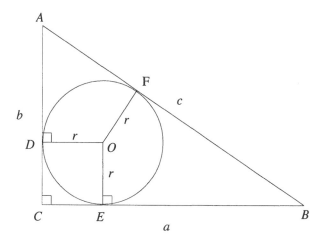

A circle, centre O and radius r, is inscribed in the right-angled triangle ABC.

Area of triangle $ABC = \frac{1}{2}ab$ and area of square $OECD = r^2$.

$ADOF$ is a kite made up of two right-angled triangles and has area $r(b-r)$ and similarly, the area of kite $BEOF$ is $r(a-r)$.

Since triangle ABC is made up of the square and the two kites:

$$\tfrac{1}{2}ab = r^2 + r(a-r) + r(b-r) \quad \Rightarrow \quad ab = 2ar + 2br - 2r^2.$$

$AD = AF$ and $BE = BF$, and so $c = a - r + b - r = a + b - 2r$.

Hence,

$$\begin{aligned} c^2 &= (a+b)^2 - 4r(a+b) + 4r^2 \\ &= a^2 + b^2 + 2ab - 4(ar + br - r^2) \\ &= a^2 + b^2, \text{using the result for } ab \text{ from above.} \end{aligned}$$

2.4 Try This

1. Explain why the areas of the kites $BEOF$ and $ADOF$ are $r(a-r)$ and $r(b-r)$ respectively.

2. Why are $AD = AF$ and $BE = BF$?

3. Explain why $c = a + b - 2r$.

4. How has the expression for c^2 been obtained?

5. Why is $2ab - 4(ar + br - r^2) = 0$?

Proof 4

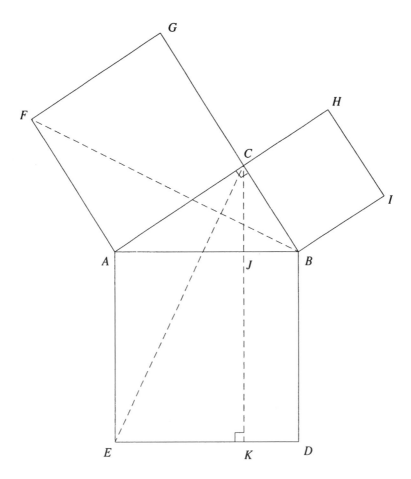

This is a simplified version of the proof given in Euclid for Pythagoras' Theorem, which appears as Proposition 47 in the *Elements*.

ABC is a triangle with a right angle at C. The perpendicular from C meets the side DE of the square on the hypotenuse of triangle ABC at K. The idea is to prove that the two rectangles into which this square is divided have the same areas as the squares on the other two sides of the triangle.

Triangle AFB has the same base and height as the square $AFGC$ and so the area of the square is twice the area of the triangle. Similarly, the area of rectangle $AEKJ$ is twice the area of triangle AEC.

The triangles AFB and ACE are congruent, since $AF = AC$, $AB = AE$ and the angles FAB and CAE are equal. Hence:

$$\text{square } AFGC = 2 \times \Delta AFB = 2 \times \Delta ACE = \text{rectangle } AEKJ.$$

Similarly:

$$\text{square } BIHC = 2 \times \Delta BIA = 2 \times \Delta BCD = \text{rectangle } BDKJ.$$

Since the two rectangles together form the square $ABDE$, it follows that:

$$\text{square } AFGC + \text{square } BIHC = \text{square } ABDE \text{ or } AB^2 = AC^2 + BC^2.$$

Proof 5

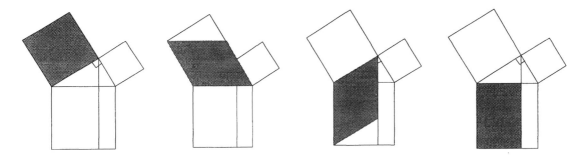

As in Euclid's proof, the square on the hypotenuse is divided into two rectangles by constructing the perpendicular to the hypotenuse and extending it across the square. It can then be shown that the areas of these rectangles are respectively equal to the areas of the squares on the other two sides, using a sequence of transformations rather than by considering congruent triangles.

The square in the left-hand diagram is transformed into the rectangle in the right-hand diagram by three successive transformations:

$$\text{shear} \quad \rightarrow \quad \text{rotation} \quad \rightarrow \quad \text{shear}.$$

A shear applied to a rectangle or parallelogram involves keeping one side fixed and moving the opposite side parallel to it. With the fixed side as base, the height, and therefore the area as well, is unchanged. Following the first shear the parallelogram is rotated through 90° clockwise. It should be clear how corresponding equal sides allow it to fit in the second position. As with the two shears, the rotation leaves the area unchanged. Since the area is invariant throughout, the areas of the square and rectangle are equal. A similar sequence of transformations, which you can produce for yourself, will show that the other square and rectangle have equal areas, to complete the proof.

Proof 6

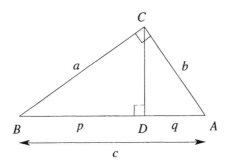

The three right-angled triangles ABC, CBD and ACD are similar.

From triangles CBD and ABC, $\cos B = \dfrac{p}{a} = \dfrac{a}{c} \implies a^2 = cp$.

From triangles ACD and ABC, $\cos A = \dfrac{q}{b} = \dfrac{b}{c} \implies b^2 = cq$.

Hence, $a^2 + b^2 = cp + cq = c(p+q) = c^2$.

Proof 7

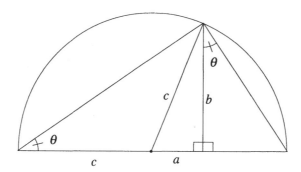

The two angles denoted by θ are equal from the property that the angle in a semi-circle is a right angle.

Then, using two similar right-angled triangles containing these angles θ:

$$\tan\theta = \frac{b}{c+a} = \frac{c-a}{b}.$$

It then follows that:

$$b^2 = (c+a)(c-a) \quad \Rightarrow \quad a^2 + b^2 = c^2.$$

Proof 8

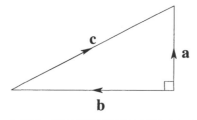

Finally, here is a proof using the scalar product of vectors which provides another interesting approach, and one which generalises readily to give the Cosine Rule. However, the ideas that underlie scalar products are sometimes introduced in a way which is dependent on Pythagoras' Theorem, so this proof is only valid if the scalar product and its properties have been derived without assuming the theorem.

$$\mathbf{c} = \mathbf{a} - \mathbf{b}$$
$$c^2 = \mathbf{c}.\mathbf{c}$$
$$= (\mathbf{a} - \mathbf{b}).(\mathbf{a} - \mathbf{b})$$
$$= \mathbf{a}.\mathbf{a} - 2\mathbf{a}.\mathbf{b} + \mathbf{b}.\mathbf{b}$$
$$= a^2 + b^2, \text{ since } \mathbf{a}.\mathbf{b} = \mathbf{0}.$$

If the right angle is replaced by a general angle θ, then $\mathbf{a}.\mathbf{b} = ab\cos\theta$ which gives the Cosine Rule:

$$c^2 = a^2 + b^2 - 2ab\cos\theta.$$

$\cos^2\theta + \sin^2\theta = 1$

$\cos^2\theta + \sin^2\theta = 1$ is one of the simplest trigonometrical identities. It is useful in a variety of topics from coordinate geometry to integration. The result follows on sensibly from the last section, since it is an immediate consequence of Pythagoras' Theorem:

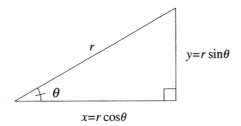

Since, $\cos\theta = \dfrac{x}{r}$ and $\sin\theta = \dfrac{y}{r}$ for any angle θ, Pythagoras' Theorem gives:

$$x^2 + y^2 = r^2 \quad \Rightarrow \quad \frac{x^2}{r^2} + \frac{y^2}{r^2} = 1 \quad \Rightarrow \quad \cos^2\theta + \sin^2\theta = 1.$$

If cosine and sine are defined from the equations $x = r\cos\theta$ and $y = r\sin\theta$ the proof is even more immediate.

It is interesting to see how the graphs of $y = \cos^2\theta$ and $y = \sin^2\theta$ are related to those of $y = \cos\theta$ and $y = \sin\theta$. This is a good example where it is worth spending some time thinking what the graphs will look like before using your graphical calculator to display them!

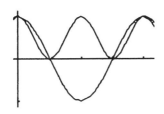   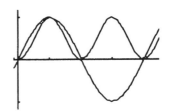

$y = \cos\theta$ and $y = \cos^2\theta$ $y = \sin\theta$ and $y = \sin^2\theta$

When the graphs of $y = \cos^2\theta$ and $y = \sin^2\theta$ are superimposed, the resulting symmetry suggests that $\cos^2\theta + \sin^2\theta = 1$.

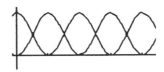

$y = \cos^2\theta$ and $y = \sin^2\theta$

2.5 Try This

There are many different ways to prove $\cos^2 \theta + \sin^2 \theta = 1$. Here are a number of further starting points for proofs of the identity.

Try proving it using these ideas.

Can you find any other proofs?

1. Differentiation

Try differentiating $\cos^2 \theta + \sin^2 \theta$. What do you notice? How does this help you?

2. Rotations

Use the rotation matrix $\begin{bmatrix} \cos \theta & -\sin \theta \\ \sin \theta & \cos \theta \end{bmatrix}$ for a rotation through an angle θ. Does the rotation change the area of a shape?

3. More rotations

What happens when you rotate a shape through an angle θ and then rotate it through an angle $-\theta$? Use rotation matrices to obtain the identity.

4. Power series

Try squaring and adding the power series:

$$\cos \theta = 1 - \frac{\theta^2}{2!} + \frac{\theta^4}{4!} - \frac{\theta^6}{6!} + \dots \quad \text{and} \quad \sin \theta = \theta - \frac{\theta^3}{3!} + \frac{\theta^5}{5!} - \frac{\theta^7}{7!} + \dots$$

5. Complex numbers

Use $e^{i\theta} = \cos \theta + i \sin \theta$ and the corresponding result for $e^{-i\theta}$.

6. Complex numbers again

Use $\cos \theta = \dfrac{e^{i\theta} + e^{-i\theta}}{2}$ and $\sin \theta = \dfrac{e^{i\theta} - e^{-i\theta}}{2i}$.

The Circle Theorems

Dynamic geometry software such as Cabri Géomètre or Geometer's Sketchpad is invaluable for exploring properties of angles in circles. The diagram below suggests the relationship between the angle at the centre of a circle and the angle at the circumference standing on the same arc. Moving the point on the circumference will suggest that all angles at the circumference standing on the same arc are equal. As with the angle sum of a triangle in the first section of this chapter, measurements on a diagram, whether made by hand or by computer, can only suggest that a general relationship is true, but being able to move points around on a circle, and to vary the circle itself, helps to provide a good feel for the situation and for the different cases that can arise.

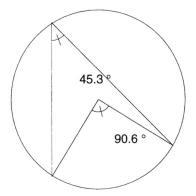
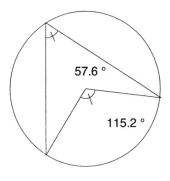

The five theorems involving angles in circles considered here are an example of a nice chain of linked results where the proof of the first provides the key to the others. This process of one result leading to others is the way in which mathematics is commonly presented in books and it reflects the way in which ideas are often developed and extended.

> 1. The angle at the centre of a circle is equal to twice the angle at the circumference standing on the same arc.

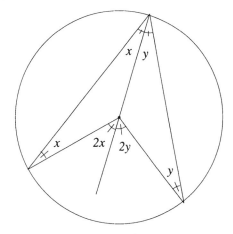

Using the angle properties of the two isosceles triangles in the diagram, the two angles at the centre of the circle are $2x$ and $2y$. The total angle at the centre is $2x + 2y$ which is twice $x + y$, the total angle at the circumference.

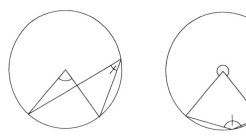
2. Angles at the circumference standing on the same arc of a circle are equal.

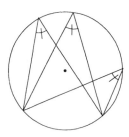

Because the angles at the circumference stand on the same arc, the angle at the centre is the same for each. Hence, by the first result, all the angles at the circumference are equal.

3. The angle in a semi-circle is a right angle.

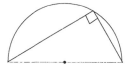

The angle at the centre is 180°, giving a right angle at the circumference, since the angle at the centre is twice the angle at the circumference for angles standing on the same arc. Alternatively the result can be proved directly as suggested in the exercise which follows.

2.7 Try This

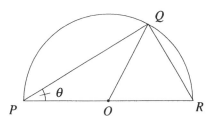

Find angle PQR in terms of angle θ by using the two isosceles triangles.

---

4. The opposite angles of a cyclic quadrilateral add up to 180°.

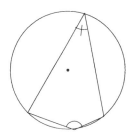

A quadrilateral is called *cyclic* when all four vertices lie on the circumference of a circle. Since the two angles at the centre add up to 360°, the corresponding opposite angles at the circumference add up to 180°.

---

5. The exterior angle of a cyclic quadrilateral is equal to the opposite interior angle.

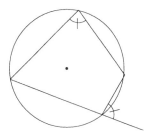

This follows from the previous result by considering the adjacent interior angle.

Trigonometric Picture Proofs

Some trigonometric results can be proved by using a picture and only brief written explanation. See if you can prove each of these results using the pictures as a guide.

2.8 Try This

1. Addition formula: $\sin(\theta + \phi) = \sin\theta\cos\phi + \cos\theta\sin\phi$.

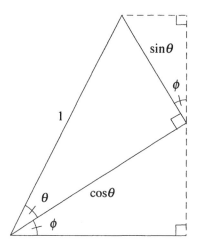

Try proving the corresponding result for $\cos(\theta + \phi)$ from the diagram.

2. Half-angle tangent formulae: $\tan\dfrac{\alpha}{2} = \dfrac{\sin\alpha}{1+\cos\alpha} = \dfrac{1-\cos\alpha}{\sin\alpha}$.

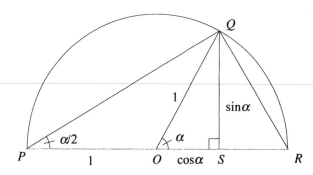

3. Sum of inverse tangents: $\tan^{-1}\dfrac{1}{2} + \tan^{-1}\dfrac{1}{3} = 45°$.

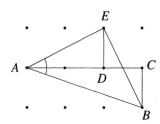

Try producing a diagram to show that $\tan^{-1}\dfrac{1}{3} = \tan^{-1}\dfrac{1}{5} + \tan^{-1}\dfrac{1}{8}$.

Some Proofs with Vectors

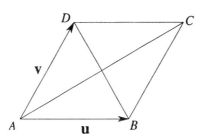

ABCD is a rhombus.

Since $\overrightarrow{AB} = \mathbf{u}$ and $\overrightarrow{AD} = \mathbf{v}$, $\overrightarrow{AC} = \mathbf{u} + \mathbf{v}$ and $\overrightarrow{DB} = \mathbf{u} - \mathbf{v}$.

Then, $\overrightarrow{AC}.\overrightarrow{DB} = (\mathbf{u} + \mathbf{v}).(\mathbf{u} - \mathbf{v}) = \mathbf{u}.\mathbf{u} + \mathbf{v}.\mathbf{u} - \mathbf{u}.\mathbf{v} - \mathbf{v}.\mathbf{v} = u^2 - v^2$, where u and v denote the magnitudes of the vectors $\mathbf{u}$ and $\mathbf{v}$.

ABCD is a rhombus with $AB = AD$ and so $u = v$.

Hence, $\overrightarrow{AC}.\overrightarrow{DB} = 0$ proving that the diagonals of the rhombus are perpendicular.

2. The medians of a triangle are concurrent.

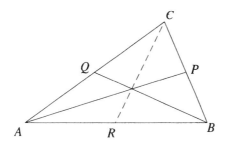

A median of a triangle is a line joining a vertex to the midpoint of the opposite side.

If $\overrightarrow{AB} = \mathbf{b}$ and $\overrightarrow{AC} = \mathbf{c}$, then $\overrightarrow{AP} = \frac{1}{2}(\mathbf{b} + \mathbf{c})$ where P is the midpoint of the side BC.

Any point on the median AP can be written as $\frac{1}{2}\lambda(\mathbf{b} + \mathbf{c})$.

Any point on the median BQ can be written as $\mathbf{b} + \mu(\frac{1}{2}\mathbf{c} - \mathbf{b})$, since $\overrightarrow{BQ} = \frac{1}{2}\mathbf{c} - \mathbf{b}$.

Since the intersection of AP and BQ lies on both, the corresponding values of λ and μ satisfy $\frac{1}{2}\lambda(\mathbf{b}+\mathbf{c}) = \mathbf{b}+\mu(\frac{1}{2}\mathbf{c}-\mathbf{b})$. Comparing the coefficients of $\mathbf{b}$ and $\mathbf{c}$ in these two expressions gives $\frac{1}{2}\lambda = 1-\mu$ and $\frac{1}{2}\lambda = \frac{1}{2}\mu$, from which it follows that $\lambda = \mu = \frac{2}{3}$.

By substituting back either of these values it follows that the two medians intersect at the point $\frac{1}{3}(\mathbf{b}+\mathbf{c})$.

This point of intersection, known as the *centroid,* divides each median in the ratio 2:1.

2.9 Try This

Show that the median from C also passes through the point $\frac{1}{3}(\mathbf{b}+\mathbf{c})$.

---

3. The altitudes of a triangle are concurrent.

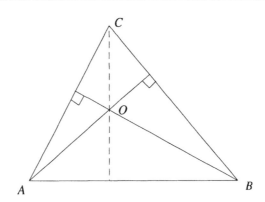

The altitude is the perpendicular height of the triangle and any triangle has three altitudes, depending which of the three sides is taken as the base. The result is trivial for a right-angled triangle, since two of the sides are altitudes.

Let the altitudes from A and B meet at O. Then, if $\overrightarrow{OA} = \mathbf{a}$, $\overrightarrow{OB} = \mathbf{b}$ and $\overrightarrow{OC} = \mathbf{c}$:

$$\overrightarrow{OA}.\overrightarrow{BC} = 0 \quad \Rightarrow \quad \mathbf{a}.(\mathbf{c}-\mathbf{b}) = 0 \quad \Rightarrow \quad \mathbf{a}.\mathbf{c} = \mathbf{a}.\mathbf{b}$$

$$\overrightarrow{OB}.\overrightarrow{CA} = 0 \quad \Rightarrow \quad \mathbf{b}.(\mathbf{a}-\mathbf{c}) = 0 \quad \Rightarrow \quad \mathbf{a}.\mathbf{b} = \mathbf{b}.\mathbf{c}.$$

Hence, $\mathbf{a}.\mathbf{c} = \mathbf{b}.\mathbf{c} \quad \Rightarrow \quad \mathbf{a}.\mathbf{c} - \mathbf{b}.\mathbf{c} = 0 \quad \Rightarrow \quad \mathbf{c}.(\mathbf{a}-\mathbf{b}) = 0 \quad \Rightarrow \quad \overrightarrow{OC}.\overrightarrow{BA} = 0.$

If the triangle is not right-angled, $\overrightarrow{OC}$ is not a zero vector. Hence, OC is perpendicular to BA and is therefore the other altitude. The three altitudes are then concurrent at O.

Chapter Three

Numbers

Would You Believe It?

Would you believe that 2=1? The 'proof' that follows looks very plausible, but clearly there must be an error somewhere! Try covering up the comments on the right and supplying them for yourself when you first read it through.

$$x = 1$$
$$x^2 = x \qquad \textit{Multiplying by } x$$
$$x^2 - 1 = x - 1 \qquad \textit{Subtracting } 1$$
$$(x-1)(x+1) = x - 1 \qquad \textit{Factorising on the left}$$
$$x + 1 = 1 \qquad \textit{Dividing by } x - 1$$
$$2 = 1 \qquad \textit{Substituting } x = 1$$

The first statement, $x = 1$, means that $x - 1 = 0$ and that the result has therefore been obtained by dividing by zero. Since division by zero is undefined, the proof is wrong.

A simpler 'proof' that 2=1, which employs the same false reasoning, goes like this.

$$0 = 0$$
$$0 \times 1 = 0 \times 2$$
$$1 = 2$$

The absurdity of dividing both sides by zero is more obvious here.

Division by zero is undefined and using a calculator to divide by zero results in an error message. One way to see why division by zero cannot be defined uses the idea of division understood as repeated subtraction. Since $12 - 3 - 3 - 3 - 3 = 0$, we say that $12 \div 3 = 4$, but $12 - 0 - 0 - 0 - 0 - \dots$ will never result in zero. No matter how many zeros are subtracted we are still left with the original 12.

Alternatively we can consider what happens to $\dfrac{12}{x}$ as $x \to 0$, by substituting smaller and smaller values for x.

$$\frac{12}{1} = 12 \qquad \frac{12}{0.1} = 120 \qquad \frac{12}{0.01} = 1200 \qquad \frac{12}{0.001} = 12000 \qquad \dots$$

Two Minuses Make a Plus

All mathematical arguments, whether they are concerned with solving a problem, deriving a formula, or proving a conjecture, consist of chains of reasoning. To ensure that an argument is correct each individual step must be valid.

For instance, here is a perfectly valid proof that the result of multiplying $^-2$ by $^-3$ is the same as multiplying 2 by 3. It demonstrates why multiplying these two negative numbers together gives a positive result, and can easily be made more general by replacing 2 and 3 by, say, a and b. The argument moves from one statement to another through a set of valid steps which can be checked by the reader.

$$^-2 \times\, ^-3 =\, ^-2 \times\, ^-3 + 0$$
$$=\, ^-2 \times\, ^-3 + 2 \times (^-3 + 3)$$
$$=\, ^-2 \times\, ^-3 + (2 \times\, ^-3 + 2 \times 3)$$
$$= (^-2 \times\, ^-3 + 2 \times\, ^-3) + 2 \times 3$$
$$= (^-2 + 2) \times\, ^-3 + 2 \times 3$$
$$= 0 + 2 \times 3$$
$$= 2 \times 3$$

However, it is not sufficient that the individual steps are valid. There must be an underlying logic to the argument. This particular example is a *deductive proof*, where you start with a correct statement and deduce from it further correct statements leading to the result that you want. Other types of proof have a different logical form, although all depend upon some deductive steps in their reasoning.

3.1 Try This

Construct a proof to show that $2 \times\, ^-3 =\, ^-2 \times 3$.

It is worth noting in conclusion here that the pattern in the $^-3$ times table makes it seem very plausible that 'two minuses make a plus' when a pair of negative numbers are multiplied.

$$3 \times\, ^-3 =\, ^-9$$
$$2 \times\, ^-3 =\, ^-6$$
$$1 \times\, ^-3 =\, ^-3$$
$$0 \times\, ^-3 = 0$$
$$^-1 \times\, ^-3 = 3$$
$$^-2 \times\, ^-3 = 6$$
$$^-3 \times\, ^-3 = 9$$

This does not, however, constitute a proof, because you should not assume that the pattern will continue in the most obvious way. Patterns are fine for suggesting conjectures, but not much use for proving them.

Odd Numbers

Consider successive sums of consecutive odd numbers.

$$1 = 1$$
$$1 + 3 = 4$$
$$1 + 3 + 5 = 9$$
$$1 + 3 + 5 + 7 = 16$$
$$1 + 3 + 5 + 7 + 9 = 25$$

The fact that the sum of the first n odd numbers is n^2, the nth square number, is made strikingly clear by a pictorial demonstration.

$$1 + 3 + 5 + 7 + \ldots + (2n - 1) = n^2$$

A preliminary step in thinking further about this is to explain why the nth odd number is given by $2n - 1$. This becomes obvious once you have noted that the nth even number is $2n$.

A simple deductive proof of the summation result involves summing corresponding pairs of terms from the sequence.

Let S be the sum of the first n consecutive odd numbers.

$$
\begin{array}{rcccccccccc}
S & = & 1 & + & 3 & + & 5 & + \ldots + & 2n-3 & + & 2n-1 \\
S & = & 2n-1 & + & 2n-3 & + & 2n-5 & + \ldots + & 3 & + & 1 \\
2S & = & 2n & + & 2n & + & 2n & + \ldots + & 2n & + & 2n
\end{array}
$$

Adding corresponding pairs gives $2S = n \times 2n = 2n^2$, and so $S = n^2$ as required.

This is just a special case of the usual proof of the formula for the sum of an arithmetic series, which states that the sum is the product of the number of terms and the mean term, both of which are n in this case.

Consecutive Numbers

> ## 3.2 Try This
>
> Choose four consecutive numbers. Calculate the product of the last pair and subtract the product of the first pair.
>
> Try this for several sets of four numbers. What do you notice about your results? Any general relationship that appears to be true is called a *conjecture*.
>
> Prove any conjectures that you make.

Three examples illustrate what is involved here:

$$4 \quad 5 \quad 6 \quad 7 \quad \rightarrow \quad 6 \times 7 - 4 \times 5 = 22$$
$$2 \quad 3 \quad 4 \quad 5 \quad \rightarrow \quad 4 \times 5 - 2 \times 3 = 14$$
$$8 \quad 9 \quad 10 \quad 11 \quad \rightarrow \quad 10 \times 11 - 8 \times 9 = 38$$

A few more examples suggest that all the answers are even and that each appears to be the sum of the four numbers (or, equivalently, double the sum of either the middle or the outer pair). This gives a conjecture which we can prove.

Four consecutive numbers can be written as $n, n+1, n+2, n+3$, which gives:

$$\text{Product of last pair} - \text{Product of first pair} = (n+2)(n+3) - n(n+1)$$
$$= (n^2 + 5n + 6) - (n^2 + n)$$
$$= 4n + 6$$
$$\text{Sum of four consecutive numbers} = n + (n+1) + (n+2) + (n+3)$$
$$= 4n + 6$$

Hence it follows that:

Product of last pair $-$ Product of first pair $=$ Sum of four consecutive numbers.

> ## 3.3 Try This
>
> With four consecutive numbers, make conjectures and prove them for:
>
> * The difference between the product of the second and fourth and the product of the first and third.
>
> * The difference between the product of the second and third and the product of the first and fourth.
>
> Prove some similar results using three or five consecutive numbers.

Prime Numbers

Prime numbers are of constant fascination to the mathematician because they are a rich source of simple results, as well as providing many very demanding and subtle problems.

One of the classic proofs in mathematics, a form of which appears in Euclid's *Elements*, shows that there are infinitely many prime numbers. This proof is particularly interesting because it is a good example of a *proof by contradiction*, or *reductio ad absurdum*.

Suppose that there is a greatest possible prime number N which completes the sequence of primes $2, 3, 5, 7, \ldots, N$.

Now consider the number, Q here denoted by , formed by the product of all these primes plus 1, namely:

$$Q = (2 \times 3 \times 5 \times 7 \times \ldots \times N) + 1.$$

Clearly dividing Q by any of the primes from 2 to N will leave a remainder of 1, so either Q is prime itself or it is divisible by a prime number between N and Q. In either case we have found a prime larger than N.

This contradicts the assumption made at the start of the proof. Therefore that assumption is false and there can be no greatest prime number. So, there are infinitely many primes.

3.4 Try This

Calculate the first few numbers of the form denoted by Q in the proof.

Which is the first number of this form that is not a prime number?

What are the factors of this number?

How does this help to explain the proof?

There is no algebraic formula for the nth prime number, but it is possible to make simple statements about the form of prime numbers. The arrangement of the prime numbers in this number array suggests a simple conjecture about their form.

1	[2]	[3]	4	[5]	6
[7]	8	9	10	[11]	12
[13]	14	15	16	[17]	18
[19]	20	21	22	[23]	24
25	26	27	28	[29]	30
[31]	32	33	34	35	36
[37]	38	39	40	[41]	42

Most of the prime numbers are confined to two columns of the six-column grid, which suggests the conjecture that:

All prime numbers except 2 and 3 are of the form $6n+1$ or $6n-1$.

This result can be proved as follows:

A set of six consecutive numbers can be written as: $6n-2$, $6n-1$, $6n$, $6n+1$, $6n+2$, $6n+3$.

Of these $6n-2$, $6n$ and $6n+2$ are even and $6n+3$ is a multiple of 3. Therefore only $6n+1$ and $6n-1$ can be primes. Thus, all primes other than 2 or 3 can be written in this form.

The *converse* of the result would state that all numbers of the form $6n+1$ or $6n-1$ are primes. It is immediately obvious from the grid that the converse is false, because there are several *counterexamples*. For example, 25 and 35 are not primes.

3.5 Try This

Prove that, with one exception, all prime numbers are of the form $4n \pm 1$.

Another simple and striking result concerns the squares of prime numbers:

The squares of all prime numbers except 2 and 3 are of the form $24n+1$.

This may be suggested by looking at numerical results, noting that a multiple of 24 does not appear when you have the square of a number that is not prime, as with $4^2 = 15+1$ or $9^2 = 80+1$.

$$2^2 = 3+1$$
$$3^2 = 8+1$$
$$5^2 = 24+1$$
$$7^2 = 48+1$$
$$11^2 = 120+1$$
$$13^2 = 168+1$$
$$17^2 = 288+1$$
$$19^2 = 360+1$$
$$23^2 = 528+1$$

A proof that the squares of all prime numbers except 2 and 3 are of the form $24n+1$ may be constructed using the factors of a difference of two squares. You should remember the factors as $a^2 - b^2 = (a+b)(a-b)$.

Consider $p^2 - 1 = (p+1)(p-1)$, where p is a prime other than 2 or 3.

p is odd and so $p-1$ and $p+1$ are consecutive even numbers. One of them is therefore a multiple of 4. It follows that $p^2 - 1$ is a multiple of 8.

Since p is not a multiple of 3, either $p-1$ or $p+1$ is a multiple of 3. It follows that $p^2 - 1$ is a multiple of 3.

$p^2 - 1$ is a multiple of both 3 and 8 and it is, therefore, a multiple of 24.

Again, the *converse* is not true: numbers of the form $24n+1$ are not always squares of primes. As a counterexample, $n = 3$ gives 73, which is not a perfect square.

Another result follows as an immediate consequence of the above, but again it might initially be suggested by looking at some numerical results.

> The difference of the squares of any two prime numbers, both greater than 3, is a multiple of 24.

$$7^2 - 5^2 = 24 \qquad 11^2 - 5^2 = 96$$
$$11^2 - 7^2 = 72 \qquad 13^2 - 7^2 = 120$$
$$13^2 - 11^2 = 48 \qquad 17^2 - 11^2 = 168$$
$$17^2 - 13^2 = 120 \qquad 19^2 - 13^2 = 192$$
$$19^2 - 17^2 = 72 \qquad 23^2 - 17^2 = 240$$
$$23^2 - 19^2 = 168 \qquad 29^2 - 19^2 = 480$$

A proof is easy to construct using the previous result.

Consider two primes p and q.

Then $p^2 = 24m + 1$ and $q^2 = 24n + 1$ for positive integers m and n.

So, $p^2 - q^2 = (24m + 1) - (24n + 1) = 24(m - n)$, which is a multiple of 24.

3.6 Try This

Prove that the difference of the squares of any two prime numbers, both greater than 3, is a multiple of 24, directly from the fact that primes other than 2 or 3 can be expressed as either $6n + 1$ or $6n - 1$.

Divisibility Tests

> A number is divisible by 4 if and only if the number formed by the last two digits is divisible by 4.

All multiples of 100 are divisible by 4, since 4 divides 100 exactly. Therefore divisibility by 4 only depends on the number formed by the last two digits. To decide if 576 is divisible by 4, you only need to know if 76 is a multiple of 4, as 500 is a multiple of 100.

The phrase 'if and only if' is often used in mathematical statements to indicate that both a result and its converse are true. The statement above says **both** 'a number is divisible by 4 if the number formed by the last two digits is divisible by 4' **and** 'the number formed by the last two digits is divisible by 4 if a number is divisible by 4'.

> **3.7 Try This**
>
> How do we test for divisibility by 2? What are the corresponding tests for divisibility by 8, 16 and other powers of 2?

$$537 \rightarrow 5+3+7=15$$
$$2895 \rightarrow 2+8+9+5=24$$

> A number is divisible by 3 if and only if the sum of its digits is also divisible by 3.

Here is a simple proof for the case of a 3-digit number:

A number with digits a, b and c can be expressed as $100a+10b+c$.

Since $100a+10b+c = 99a+9b+a+b+c$, it follows that $100a+10b+c$ is divisible by 3 if and only if $a+b+c$ is divisible by 3.

A general proof can be constructed similarly for a number with any number of digits:

A number with digits $a_n, a_{n-1}, \ldots a_1, a_0$ can be expressed as:

$$N = 10^n a_n + 10^{n-1} a_{n-1} + \ldots + 10a_1 + a_0.$$

Since $10^n - 1$ is divisible by 3 for any value of n (consider 9, 99, 999, 9999 and so on), we can write

$$N = (10^n - 1)a_n + (10^{n-1} - 1)a_{n-1} + \ldots + (10-1)a_1 + a_0 + a_n + a_{n-1} + \ldots + a_1$$

Hence N is divisible by 3 if and only if $a_n + a_{n-1} + \ldots + a_1 + a_0$ is divisible by 3.

A number is divisible by 9 if and only if the sum of its digits is also divisible by 9.

The corresponding test for divisibility by 9 can be proved by substituting 9 for 3 throughout in the two previous proofs.

3.8 Try This

What do you notice about these 3-digit multiples of 11?

$$110, 121, 132, 143, 154, \ldots, 264, 275, 286, 297, \ldots$$

The sequence continues 308, 319, 330, ...

Does what you noted still apply? How do you test 3-digit numbers for divisibility by 11?

Prove your test for divisibility by 11 for 3-digit numbers.

Extend the idea to numbers with more digits.

Divisibility

$9^n - 1$ is a multiple of 8 for any positive integer n.

A look at a few numerical cases is not particularly suggestive and provides slender evidence for making the conjecture above!

$$9^1 - 1 = 8$$
$$9^2 - 1 = 80$$
$$9^3 - 1 = 728$$
$$9^4 - 1 = 6560$$

There are many ways of proving this. It is often instructive to consider alternatives, so four different proofs are considered here.

Proof 1

$9^n - 1 = 3^{2n} - 1 = (3^n - 1)(3^n + 1)$, using the difference of two squares.

Since 3^n is odd, $3^n - 1$ and $3^n + 1$ are consecutive even numbers and hence one is divisible by 2 and the other by 4.

It follows that $9^n - 1$ is a multiple of 8 for any positive integer n.

Proof 2

If $n = 1$, then $9^1 - 1 = 8$ which is certainly a multiple of 8.

Suppose that the result is true for $n = k$.

Then $9^k - 1 = 8a$, where a is a positive integer, and so:

$$9^{k+1} - 1 = 9 \times 9^k - 1$$
$$= 9(8a + 1) - 1$$
$$= 72a + 8$$
$$= 8(9a + 1), \text{which is a multiple of 8.}$$

Hence, if $9^n - 1$ is a multiple of 8 then so is $9^{n+1} - 1$. Since the result is true for $n = 1$, then, by *induction*, it is true for all positive integers n.

Proof 3

Using the binomial theorem,

$$9^n = (8 + 1)^n$$
$$= 8^n + {}^nC_1 8^{n-1} 1^1 + {}^nC_2 8^{n-2} 1^2 + \ldots + {}^nC_{n-1} 8^1 1^{n-1} + 1^n$$
$$= 8(8^{n-1} + {}^nC_1 8^{n-2} + {}^nC_2 8^{n-3} + \ldots + {}^nC_{n-1}) + 1$$
$$= 8a + 1, \text{ where } a \text{ is a positive integer.}$$

Hence $9^n - 1$ is a multiple of 8 for any positive integer n.

Proof 4

Since $x^n - 1 = (x - 1)(x^{n-1} + x^{n-2} + \ldots + x + 1)$, then $x^n - 1$ is divisible by $x - 1$.

Hence with $x = 9$, $9^n - 1$ is a multiple of $9 - 1 = 8$.

Proof 1 is a neat argument for the particular example, but it only extends to a few other cases involving square numbers, such as proving that $4^n - 1$ is a multiple of 3. This method is not much help, however, in proving that $5^n - 1$ is a multiple of 4.

It is interesting to see how the inductive proof in the second case works. Although it generalises readily, it is certainly not the most straightforward approach. The method of proof 3 also extends readily to other cases.

Proof 4 has the advantage of being very short and easy to follow, and is a good example where proving a more general result is simpler than looking at an individual case.

Note that the *converse* is not true, because if $9^n - 1$ is a multiple of 8, then n is not always an integer. For example, if $9^n - 1 = 16$, n lies somewhere between 2 and 3.

The Irrationality of $\sqrt{2}$

For many, the idea of an irrational number is not a simple one. In simple terms, rational numbers are what most people describe as fractions, and their decimal representations are either terminating or recurring. Irrational numbers are those numbers that cannot be represented in either of these ways and their decimal representations are both non-terminating and non-recurring. Familiar members of this family are $\sqrt{2}$, $\sqrt[3]{5}$ and most other roots, π and e.

The fact that $\sqrt{2}$ is an irrational number was one of the key problems that puzzled Greek mathematicians over two thousand years ago. Here we give two proofs by contradiction. The first is the classic one from Euclid, referred to in Hardy's *A Mathematician's Apology*, along with the proof of the infinite number of primes, as good examples of mathematical beauty. The second, which is simpler and just as elegant, comes from Davis and Hersh's *The Mathematical Experience*.

Proof 1

Suppose that $\sqrt{2} = \dfrac{p}{q}$, where p and q are positive integers with no common factor.

Then $p^2 = 2q^2$ which implies that p^2 is *even* and therefore that p is also *even*.

So let $p = 2r$ so that $4r^2 = 2q^2$.

This gives $q^2 = 2r^2$ which implies that q is also *even*.

Since p and q cannot both be even, the original assumption must be false.

Proof 2

As in proof 1, suppose that $\sqrt{2} = \dfrac{p}{q}$, where p and q are positive integers with no common factor. As before, $p^2 = 2q^2$.

Now p^2, as a square number, has an *even* number of prime factors, but $2q^2$ has an *odd* number of prime factors, which is a contradiction. So the original assumption is false.

3.9 Try This

Prove the irrationality of $\sqrt{3}$ and $\sqrt[3]{2}$ in similar ways.

What happens if this method of proof is applied to $\sqrt{9}$?

Chapter Four

Algebra

The Quadratic Equation Formula

$$\text{If } ax^2 + bx + c = 0 \text{ and } a \neq 0, \text{ then } x = \frac{-b \pm \sqrt{b^2 - 4ac}}{2a}.$$

The formula for the roots of a quadratic equation is usually proved by completing the square. The first proof simplifies this usual method by considering the case where $a = 1$ first. The second proof uses the symmetry of the quadratic curve to suggest the algebraic form of the roots. The third uses the coordinates of the minimum point found by examining the properties of some families of quadratic curves plotted using a graphical calculator or a graph plotter.

1. Completing the square

It often helps, in understanding the structure of a general algebraic argument, to look at a particular case first.

$$x^2 + 6x + 4 = 0$$

$x^2 + 6x = -4$	*Subtracting 4 from both sides*
$x^2 + 6x + 9 = -4 + 9$	*Adding 9 to complete the square*
$(x + 3)^2 = 5$	*Simplifying*
$x + 3 = \pm\sqrt{5}$	*Taking square root*
$x = -3 \pm \sqrt{5}$	*Subtracting 3*

This argument is now repeated using a more general case where 6 is replaced by b and 4 is replaced by c. To keep things simple the coefficient of x^2 is still 1.

$$x^2 + bx + c = 0$$

$x^2 + bx = -c$	*Subtracting c from both sides*
$x^2 + bx + \dfrac{b^2}{4} = -c + \dfrac{b^2}{4}$	*Adding $\dfrac{b^2}{4}$ to complete the square*
$(x + \dfrac{b}{2})^2 = \dfrac{b^2 - 4c}{4}$	*Simplifying*
$x + \dfrac{b}{2} = \dfrac{\pm\sqrt{b^2 - 4c}}{2}$	*Taking square root*
$x = \dfrac{-b \pm \sqrt{b^2 - 4c}}{2}$	*Subtracting $\dfrac{b}{2}$*

2. Using symmetry

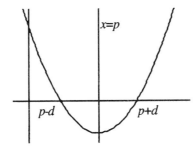

From the graph of a quadratic function with two distinct roots, it is evident that the roots are equally spaced on either side of the line of symmetry. So, if the line of symmetry is $x = p$, the roots are $p + d$ and $p - d$ for some number $d \neq 0$.

Consider now the quadratic function $f(x) = ax^2 + bx + c$.

$f(x) = 0$ when $x = p + d$ and when $x = p - d$ and so it follows that:

$$f(p + d) = 0 \quad \Rightarrow \quad a(p + d)^2 + b(p + d) + c = 0.$$

$$f(p - d) = 0 \quad \Rightarrow \quad a(p - d)^2 + b(p - d) + c = 0.$$

You can verify that multiplying out and then subtracting these two equations gives:

$$4apd + 2bd = 0 \quad \Rightarrow \quad p = \frac{-b}{2a}, \text{ since } d \neq 0.$$

It can then be shown that $d = \dfrac{\pm\sqrt{b^2 - 4ac}}{2a}$ and so the roots are $x = \dfrac{-b \pm \sqrt{b^2 - 4ac}}{2a}$.

3. Finding the minimum point

A graphical calculator or a graph plotter is very useful for looking at families of curves. These often suggest links between the form of the equations and properties of the curves. The two examples illustrated here suggest the form that the minimum point takes for a quadratic function and provide an alternative to the usual approach using calculus. By linking this with the completed squares form of the quadratic function, the formula for the roots of a quadratic equation can be obtained.

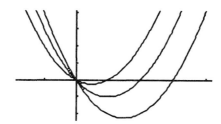

This diagram shows graphs of $y = x^2 + bx$ for $b = -1$, $b = -2$ and $b = -3$.

Since $y = x^2 + bx$ meets the x axis at 0 and $-b$, the symmetry of the curves immediately suggests that the line of symmetry is $x = -\dfrac{b}{2}$.

Substituting this value of x into the equation of the curve gives the y coordinate of the minimum point as:

$$y = \frac{b^2}{4} - \frac{b^2}{2} = -\frac{b^2}{4}.$$

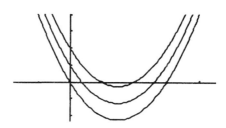

This diagram shows graphs of $y = x^2 + bx + c$ for $b = -3$ with $c = 0$, $c = 1$ and $c = 2$.

The line of symmetry is not altered as c is varied for a given value of b. It follows that the minimum point is given by $x = -\dfrac{b}{2}$ and $y = -\dfrac{b^2}{4} + c = \dfrac{4c - b^2}{4}$.

Now the graph of the function $y = (x - p)^2 + q$ has a minimum point at (p, q).

The equation $(x - p)^2 + q = 0$ has solutions $x = p \pm \sqrt{-q}$. Substituting the coordinates found for the minimum point for p and q then gives the result, which can be extended to the general case in the way suggested previously.

$$x = p \pm \sqrt{-q} = \frac{-b}{2} \pm \sqrt{\frac{b^2 - 4c}{4}} = \frac{-b \pm \sqrt{b^2 - 4c}}{2}.$$

Pascal's Triangle

Pascal's Triangle is a familiar way of displaying the values of ^nC_r, where ^nC_r is interpreted as the number of ways of choosing r items from n different items. ^nC_r is evaluated using the formula $^nC_r = \dfrac{n!}{r!(n-r)!}$, where r and n are non-negative integers with $n \geq r$.

^nC_r is often written in the alternative form $\dbinom{n}{r}$. The two forms are equivalent for the values of n considered here, but the latter is in fact defined differently, and for a wider range of values of n.

^nC_r	0	1	2	3	4	5
0	1					
1	1	1				
2	1	2	1			
3	1	3	3	1		
4	1	4	6	4	1	
5	1	5	10	10	5	1

The symmetry in the numbers of each line is explained by noting that the number of ways of choosing r items from n is the same as the number of ways of choosing $n - r$ items from n, reflecting the fact that $^nC_r = {}^nC_{n-r}$.

4.3 Try This

By considering what happens when $n = r$, what is the value of $0!$?

PASCAL (1623 - 1662)

Blaise Pascal, who was born at Clermont in France, is remembered particularly for the triangular array of numbers named after him. The triangle was known to the Chinese at least 500 years before Pascal's time, but he pursued its links with probability which was one of his major areas of interest. His other work related chiefly to geometry and included Pascal's Theorem which states that, for any hexagon inscribed in a conic section, the three intersection points of opposite pairs of sides lie in a straight line.

The key property of Pascal's Triangle is that the sum of each pair of consecutive numbers in a line gives a number in the line below. This can be used for generating successive lines.

For example, you can see from the table that $^4C_2 + {}^4C_3 = 6 + 4 = 10 = {}^5C_3$, and it is true if $r > 0$ that $^nC_{r-1} + {}^nC_r = {}^{n+1}C_r$. Here is a proof of this general result.

$$
\begin{aligned}
^nC_{r-1} + {}^nC_r &= \frac{n!}{(r-1)!(n-r+1)!} + \frac{n!}{r!(n-r)!} \\
&= \frac{n!r}{r!(n-r+1)!} + \frac{n!(n-r+1)}{r!(n-r+1)!}, \quad \text{since } r! = r(r-1)! \text{ if } r > 0 \\
&= \frac{n!(r+n-r+1)}{r!(n-r+1)!} \\
&= \frac{(n+1)!}{r!(n+1-r)!} \\
&= {}^{n+1}C_r
\end{aligned}
$$

The Arithmetic and Geometric Means Inequality

The *arithmetic mean* of two numbers a and b is given by $x = \frac{1}{2}(a+b)$, where a, x and b form an arithmetic sequence with x half-way between a and b. The fact that $x - a = b - x$ leads to the formula for x.

If the three numbers a, y and b form a geometric sequence then ratios, rather than differences, are equal. In this case $\frac{y}{a} = \frac{b}{y}$, giving $y = \sqrt{ab}$, the *geometric mean*.

A simple numerical example illustrates some characteristics of these two means:

Suppose the population of a city was 1 million in 1985 and 2 million in 1995. Estimate the population in 1990.

The *arithmetic mean* is $\frac{1}{2}(1+2)$ giving 1.5 million and would answer the question if linear growth of the population was assumed.

The *geometric mean* is $\sqrt{1 \times 2}$ giving about 1.4 million, which assumes exponential growth, possibly a more realistic assumption.

The numerical example suggests that the arithmetic mean of a pair of non-negative numbers is greater than their geometric mean. This is true in general, except that the means are equal when the two numbers are equal.

> If a and b are two non-negative numbers, then $\frac{1}{2}(a+b) \geq \sqrt{ab}$.

Attempts to prove this statement often produce an argument like that given below.

$$\frac{1}{2}(a+b) \geq \sqrt{ab}$$

$$\frac{1}{4}(a+b)^2 \geq ab$$

$$(a+b)^2 \geq 4ab$$

$$a^2 + 2ab + b^2 \geq 4ab$$

$$a^2 - 2ab + b^2 \geq 0$$

$$(a-b)^2 \geq 0$$

This argument starts with the statement which is to be proved. It then proceeds by a set of valid steps to the final statement. The final statement is certainly true, because the square of any number is greater than or equal to zero. On this basis some might argue that the initial statement must therefore be true. However, the proof is not acceptable because it starts by assuming the truth of what you are trying to prove.

You could easily prove that $1 = 2$ in this way by reversing the argument considered in the previous chapter!

$$1 = 2$$

$$0 \times 1 = 0 \times 2$$

$$0 = 0$$

The first statement is what you are trying to prove. The final statement is obviously true. The steps in between are valid, because both sides have been multiplied by zero, not divided. Obviously there is something wrong. The error lies in assuming, at the beginning of the argument, that what you have to prove is known to be true.

> In a *deductive proof* the argument must start from something that is true, not from the statement that you are trying to prove. You have to start from firm ground and proceed from there to demonstrate that your result follows logically.

Commonly, the inequality concerning the arithmetic and geometric means of two non-negative numbers is proved by reversing the steps of the argument given earlier.

$$(a-b)^2 \geq 0$$
$$a^2 - 2ab + b^2 \geq 0$$
$$a^2 + 2ab + b^2 \geq 4ab$$
$$(a+b)^2 \geq 4ab$$
$$\tfrac{1}{4}(a+b)^2 \geq ab$$
$$\tfrac{1}{2}(a+b) \geq \sqrt{ab}$$

Note that the final step is valid because both sides are non-negative. The first statement is certainly true and the individual steps in the argument are all valid, so the proof is valid. However, quite justifiably, it might be wondered what prompts you to start with $(a-b)^2 \geq 0$. Surely it is only prompted through considering the incorrect reverse argument, so that it looks like 'working backwards from the answer'?

It is actually often very sensible to try 'working backwards from the answer' when solving mathematical problems, because this can often give clues as to a suitable way of proceeding in the way that is evident here. However, it is essential that the final argument is written the right way round.

This leads on very nicely to *proof by contradiction*. Such a proof starts with what you are trying to prove and looks at what happens if you assume that it is not true. So, in this case, we assume that $\tfrac{1}{2}(a+b) < \sqrt{ab}$ or, in other words, that the arithmetic mean is strictly less than the geometric mean. We then follow through the consequences of this assumption. The steps are as in the original argument, except that the inequality has changed.

$$\tfrac{1}{2}(a+b) < \sqrt{ab}$$
$$\tfrac{1}{4}(a+b)^2 < ab$$
$$(a+b)^2 < 4ab$$
$$a^2 + 2ab + b^2 < 4ab$$
$$a^2 - 2ab + b^2 < 0$$
$$(a-b)^2 < 0$$

Note that the first step is valid because only non-negative values have been squared. Clearly the final statement $(a-b)^2 < 0$ is false – a contradiction – so the initial statement $\tfrac{1}{2}(a+b) < \sqrt{ab}$ must also be false. Hence $\tfrac{1}{2}(a+b) \geq \sqrt{ab}$ must be true. Although the logical structure of the argument is more difficult than with a deductive proof, there is perhaps some psychological advantage in such a case in starting from a statement that is directly related to what has to be proved.

To end this section on a more intuitive note, here are three ways of demonstrating pictorially the truth of the inequality concerning the arithmetic and geometric means.

Proof 1

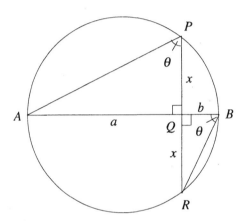

PR is a chord perpendicular to the diameter AB of the circle. Q is the point where the chord meets the diameter. The distances AQ and BQ are denoted by a and b respectively, and the equal lengths PQ and QR are denoted by x. The angles APQ and RBQ are equal angles in the same segment denoted by θ. It follows, by considering the right-angled triangles AQP and RQB, that:

$$\tan \theta = \frac{a}{x} = \frac{x}{b} \quad \Rightarrow \quad x^2 = ab \quad \Rightarrow \quad x = \sqrt{ab}.$$

The radius of the circle is $\tfrac{1}{2}(a+b)$ and hence, since PQ is less than or equal to the radius, it follows that $\tfrac{1}{2}(a+b) \geq \sqrt{ab}$.

Proof 2

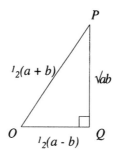

In a right-angled triangle OPQ, let $OP = \frac{1}{2}(a+b)$ and $OQ = \frac{1}{2}(a-b)$.

Then, applying Pythagoras' Theorem to the triangle, the perpendicular height PQ is:

$$\sqrt{\left(\tfrac{1}{2}(a+b)\right)^2 - \left(\tfrac{1}{2}(a-b)\right)^2} = \sqrt{ab}.$$

Since the hypotenuse OP is always greater than the perpendicular PQ, except for equality in the extreme case where hypotenuse and perpendicular coincide, it follows that:

$$\tfrac{1}{2}(a+b) \geq \sqrt{ab}.$$

Proof 3

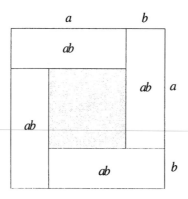

In this picture, four rectangles of length a and width b are arranged to form a square with edges of length $a+b$. The inner square has edges of length $a-b$. The area of the larger square is greater than the area of the four rectangles, except in the case where the rectangles are squares when $a = b$, and so:

$$(a+b)^2 \geq 4ab \quad \Rightarrow \quad \tfrac{1}{2}(a+b) \geq \sqrt{ab}.$$

Proof by Induction

We all know that 'one thing leads to another'. Well, this is the underlying principle of induction – if it can be shown that the truth of one case leads to the truth of the next case, then it only remains to prove a first case to prove the result for all cases. A commonly used analogy is that if you are:

- able to get onto the first stair, and

- able to get from any stair to the next stair, then

- you can climb the staircase.

Proofs by induction are useful in proving general results which consist of successive cases corresponding to the integers $1, 2, 3, \dots n$. This often involves series, but also can involve divisibility, results in calculus and other situations where a sequence of cases is generated. A proof by induction offers little insight into where a result comes from – it is necessary to make a conjecture first and then prove it, whereas deduction can actually generate a new result.

A proof by induction consists of three parts:

- Firstly, show that the result holds for a first case, usually $n = 1$.

- Secondly, suppose that the result is true for a certain value, greater than or equal to the first case, and show that this leads by deductive proof to it holding for the next value also.

- Finally, putting these two parts together, you conclude that the result is true for all cases of n greater than or equal to the first case.

Example 1

n	1	2	3	4	5
$5^n + 3$	8	28	128	628	3128

It looks plausible from the five results in the table above that $5^n + 3$ is always divisible by 4. A proof of this result provides a simple example of a proof by induction.

The result is certainly true for $n = 1$, so suppose it is true for $n = k$, where $k \geq 1$:

Suppose, then, that $5^k + 3$ is divisible by 4 and consider $5^{k+1} + 3$, the case where $n = k + 1$.

Since $5^{k+1} + 3 = 5(5^k + 3) - 12$, it follows that $5^{k+1} + 3$ is divisible by 4, because 12 is certainly divisible by 4 and it has been assumed that $5^k + 3$ is divisible by 4.

So, if the result is true for $n = k$ then it is true for $n = k + 1$. Since it is true for $n = 1$, it must then be true for all positive integer values of n.

Note that the result is also true for $n = 0$, so this could have been used as the first case.

Example 2

$$1 = 1$$
$$1 + 2 = 3$$
$$1 + 2 + 3 = 6$$
$$1 + 2 + 3 + 4 = 10$$
$$1 + 2 + 3 + 4 + 5 = 15$$

The formula, $\sum_{r=1}^{n} r = \tfrac{1}{2}n(n+1)$, for the sum of the first n natural numbers, or, equivalently, the nth triangular number, is well known. Proving this result by induction provides a good simple example of the procedure.

Here is a proof by induction that $\sum_{r=1}^{n} r = \tfrac{1}{2}n(n+1)$.

The result holds for $n = 1$, since the left-hand side and the right-hand side are both equal to 1.

Suppose that the result is true for some fixed integer value of n, say $n = k$, so that:

$$\sum_{r=1}^{k} r = \tfrac{1}{2}k(k+1).$$

Adding $k + 1$ to both sides gives:

$$\sum_{r=1}^{k+1} r = \tfrac{1}{2}k(k+1) + (k+1).$$

The right-hand side is simplified by factorising to give an expression with the same form as the original, but with $k + 1$ in place of k:

$$\sum_{r=1}^{k+1} r = \tfrac{1}{2}(k+1)(k+2).$$

Thus, if the result is true for $n = k$, then it is true for $n = k + 1$. Since it is true for $n = 1$, then, by induction, it is true for all positive integer values of n

Consider a wrong alternative formula for the triangular numbers: $\sum_{r=1}^{n} r = \frac{1}{12}(n^3 + 17n - 6)$.

This certainly works for $n = 1$, since $\frac{1}{12}(1 + 17 - 6) = 1$.

Assuming that it works for $n = k$ and adding on the next term gives:

$$\sum_{r=1}^{k+1} r = \frac{1}{12}(k^3 + 17k - 6) + (k+1) = \frac{1}{12}(k^3 + 29k + 6).$$

However, substituting $k + 1$ in place of k in the formula gives:

$$\sum_{r=1}^{k+1} r = \frac{1}{12}\left((k+1)^3 + 17(k+1) - 6\right) = \frac{1}{12}(k^3 + 3k^2 + 20k + 12).$$

This provides an example of what happens when induction is applied to a false result. The two expressions are certainly not the same, so the formula cannot be correct. In fact the formula is true for $n = 1$, $n = 2$ and $n = 3$, but it fails for $n = 4$. Finding that $n = 4$ is a counterexample is, of course, much simpler than showing that the inductive step goes wrong!

Example 3

y	x	x^2	x^3	x^4
$\dfrac{dy}{dx}$	1	$2x$	$3x^2$	$4x^3$

At an early stage in learning about derivatives, before you learn about the product rule, you note the pattern in the results above for the first few integer powers of x, and arrive at the general result $\frac{d}{dx}(x^n) = nx^{n-1}$. This gives another example of proof by induction.

The result holds for $k = 1$, since $\frac{d}{dx}(x^1) = 1$ and $1x^0 = 1$.

If the result is true for some fixed integer value of n, say $n = k$, then $\frac{d}{dx}(x^k) = kx^{k-1}$.

Using the product rule gives: $\frac{d}{dx}(x^{k+1}) = \frac{d}{dx}(x^k.x) = x.kx^{k-1} + x^k.1 = (k+1)x^k$.

The right-hand expression has the same form as the original, but with $k + 1$ in place of k. Thus, if the result is true for $n = k$, then it is true for $n = k + 1$. Since it is true for $n = 1$, then, by induction, it is true for all positive integer values of n.

Example 4

The Fibonacci Sequence is well known. Apart from the first two terms which are given, each term of the Fibonacci Sequence is generated by adding the two previous terms. Denoting the nth term by F_n, this property can be expressed as $F_n = F_{n-1} + F_{n-2}$ for $n > 2$.

The sequence has many simple and surprising properties – the table which follows gives successive sums of the series formed from the sequence.

i	1	2	3	4	5	6	7	8	9	10
F_i	1	1	2	3	5	8	13	21	34	55
$\sum_{i=1}^{n} F_i$	1	2	4	7	12	20	33	54	88	143

It is easy to spot that each number in the bottom row is 1 less than the number which is two to the right in the row above.

This conjecture, that the sum of the first n terms of the Fibonacci Sequence is given by $\sum_{i=1}^{n} F_i = F_{n+2} - 1$, can be proved by induction:

The result is true for $n = 1$, since $F_3 - 1 = 2 - 1 = 1 = F_1$.

Suppose the result is true for $n = k$: $\sum_{i=1}^{k} F_i = F_{k+2} - 1$.

Since $F_{k+3} = F_{k+2} + F_{k+1}$, the result for $n = k + 1$ follows by adding the next term:

$$\sum_{i=1}^{k+1} F_i = \sum_{i=1}^{k} F_i + F_{k+1} = F_{k+2} - 1 + F_{k+1} = F_{k+3} - 1 = F_{(k+1)+2} - 1.$$

Hence, if the result is true for $n = k$, then it is true for $n = k + 1$. Since it is true for $n = 1$, by induction, it is true for all positive integer values of n.

FIBONACCI (1175? - 1240)

Leonardo Fibonacci was born in Pisa in Italy. His most famous work, the *Liber Abaci*, considered the advantages of the Arabic number system over the system of Roman numbers. The book discusses many algebraic ideas and looks at a wide range of problems, including the rabbit problem which gives the famous sequence:

How many pairs of rabbits will be produced in a year, beginning with a single pair, if, in every month, each pair bears a new pair which is productive from the second month on?

Example 5

$$(1+x)^0 = 1$$
$$(1+x)^1 = 1+x$$
$$(1+x)^2 = 1+2x+x^2$$
$$(1+x)^3 = 1+3x+3x^2+x^3$$
$$(1+x)^3 = 1+4x+6x^2+4x^3+x^4$$

The coefficients in the expansions of powers of the binomial expression $1+x$ are familiar as the numbers in Pascal's Triangle. The individual binomial coefficients of x^r in $(1+x)^n$ are denoted by ^nC_r or $\begin{pmatrix} n \\ r \end{pmatrix}$ and can be evaluated as $\dfrac{n!}{r!(n-r)!}$, noting that $0!=1$.

Each coefficient is obtained by adding the coefficient immediately above to the one on its left. This enables you to work out successive terms in a simple way. The property, discussed earlier in the chapter, is expressed symbolically as $^nC_r+{}^nC_{r-1}={}^{n+1}C_r$ where $r>0$.

The binomial theorem for non-negative integer values of n can be stated as:

$$(1+x)^n = 1+{}^nC_1x+{}^nC_2x^2+...+{}^nC_nx^n$$

Here is a proof by induction.

When $n=1$, both sides give $1+x$ so the result is true for $n=1$.

Suppose that the theorem is true for $n=k$.

$$(1+x)^k = 1+{}^kC_1x+{}^kC_2x^2+...+{}^kC_kx^k.$$

Now multiply both sides by $(1+x)$.

$$(1+x)^{k+1} = (1+{}^kC_1x+{}^kC_2x^2+...+x^k)(1+x)$$
$$= 1+\left({}^kC_1+1\right)x+\left({}^kC_1+{}^kC_2\right)x^2+...+x^{k+1}$$
$$= 1+{}^{k+1}C_1x+{}^{k+1}C_2x^2+...+x^{k+1}$$

The bracketed terms on the second line simplify to give the coefficients on the third line using the Pascal Triangle property $^kC_r+{}^kC_{r-1}={}^{k+1}C_r$.

So, if the result is true for $n=k$ then it is true for $n=k+1$. Since it is true for $n=1$, then, by induction, it is true for all positive integer values of n.

Example 6

The angle sum of a convex n-sided polygon is $(n-2)180°$. Although not the simplest way to prove this result (see chapter 2), it is worth seeing induction applied to a result which is not true for all positive integer values of n.

The result is true for $n = 3$, because the angle sum of a triangle is $180°$, but it is obviously not meaningful for either $n = 1$ or $n = 2$.

Suppose that the result is true for $n = k$, so that the angle sum is $(k-2)180°$.

A $(k+1)$-sided polygon is equivalent to a k-sided polygon with a triangle placed on one of its sides. This increases the angle sum by $180°$ to give:

$$(k-2)180° + 180° = ((k+1) - 2)180°$$

So, if the result is true for $n = k$, then it is true for $n = k+1$. Since it is true for $n = 3$, then, by induction, it is true for all positive integer values of $n \geq 3$.

4.5 Try This

Try proving the following results by induction:

1. $\displaystyle\sum_{r=1}^{n} r^2 = \tfrac{1}{6}n(n+1)(2n+1)$.

2. $n^3 + 2n$ is divisible by 3 for all positive integer values of n.

3. $\displaystyle\sum_{i=1}^{n} F_i^2 = F_n F_{n+1}$, where F_i is the nth term of the Fibonacci Sequence.

4. $\dfrac{1}{1.2} + \dfrac{1}{2.3} + \dfrac{1}{3.4} + ... + \dfrac{1}{n(n+1)} = \dfrac{n}{n+1}$.

5. $\dfrac{d}{dx}(x^{-n}) = -nx^{-n-1}$ for all positive integer values of n.

6. $2^n > 2n$ for $n > 2$.

It is usually assumed that the major difficulty with a proof by induction lies in the often complicated algebra of the second part. However, identifying and appreciating the error in the following fallacious proof provides a much sterner test of understanding.

> All the people in any set of size n are of the same height.

The result is certainly true for $n = 1$, because one person is the same height as herself or himself.

Now, suppose that the result is true for any set of size k, and consider what happens when an extra person joins the set and increases it by 1 to give $k + 1$.

All the people in any subset of size k taken from the set of $k + 1$ people are of the same height, according to our assumption. It follows that the set of $k + 1$ people must all be of the same height.

The result is true for $n = 1$, and, if true for $n = k$, it is true for $n = k + 1$, and so the conditions for a proof by induction have been fulfilled.

> ### 4.6 Try This
>
> Clearly all people cannot be the same height.
>
> Where, then, is the fallacy in the proof?

Chapter Five

Calculus

Calculus and Circles

The formula for the area of a circle, $A = \pi r^2$, is familiar. It is interesting to consider some different ways of demonstrating why it is plausible. Upper and lower bounds for the area of the circle can be determined quite easily from the following diagram.

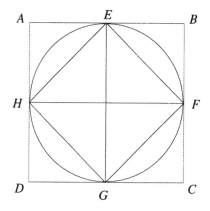

A circle of radius r is inscribed in the square $ABCD$ and the square $EFGH$ is inscribed in the circle as shown. The area of the circle clearly lies between the areas of the squares.

$ABCD$ is made up of 4 squares each of area r^2, giving the area of $ABCD$ as $4r^2$.

$EFGH$ is made up of 4 triangles each of area $\frac{1}{2}r^2$, giving the area of $EFGH$ as $2r^2$.

It follows that $2r^2 < \text{area of circle} < 4r^2$.

5.1 Try This

Show that the area of a regular dodecagon (12 sides) inscribed in a circle of radius r is $3r^2$.

Show that the area of a regular octagon (8 sides) with a circle of radius r inscribed is $8(\sqrt{2} - 1)r^2$.

Now explain why $3r^2 < \text{area of circle} < 3.32r^2$.

A circle can be divided up into a large number of sectors. The sum of the arc lengths of these sectors is equal to the circumference of the circle. The area of a narrow sector can be approximated by the area of a triangle with the arc length as base and the radius of the circle as height. The formula for the area of a circle is obtained by considering the limit as the number of sectors tends to infinity. The argument seems very plausible and certainly leads to the correct result, but it is important to treat such arguments with caution. The argument needs some refinement if it is to be acceptable as an adequate proof. Some examples in the final chapter highlight the dangers of arguments using limits.

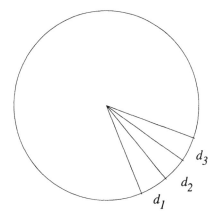

Area of circle $\approx \frac{1}{2}d_1r + \frac{1}{2}d_2r + \frac{1}{2}d_3r + ... = \frac{1}{2}r(d_1 + d_2 + d_3 + ...)$.

As the number of sectors is increased, $d_1 + d_2 + d_3 + ... \rightarrow 2\pi r$, the circumference of the circle.

Hence, area of circle $= \frac{1}{2}r.2\pi r = \pi r^2$.

A similar argument leads to the formula for the area of a sector of a circle of radius r and angle θ, measured in radians. In this case $d_1 + d_2 + d_3 + ... \rightarrow r\theta$, the arc length of the sector, which then gives area of sector $= \frac{1}{2}r.r\theta = \frac{1}{2}r^2\theta$. The full circle is, of course, the special case where $\theta = 2\pi$.

The formula for the area of a sector of a graph, whose equation is given in polar form, is $\int_{\theta_1}^{\theta_2} \frac{1}{2}r^2 d\theta$. This is an immediate extension of the result for the area of a sector.

5.2 Try This

Given that the formula for the surface area of a sphere is $4\pi r^2$, prove that the volume of a sphere is given by the formula $\frac{4}{3}\pi r^3$ by dividing the sphere into solid 'sectors' which can be approximated as pyramids.

Reminder: Volume of a pyramid $= \frac{1}{3}$ area of base $\times$ height.

You might expect to be able to prove an area formula using calculus. The following two calculus proofs give the formula for the area of a circle and, by way of comparison, the formula for the volume of a sphere.

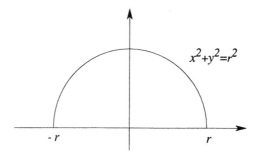

$$x^2 + y^2 = r^2$$

The equation of a circle, with centre at the origin and radius r, is $x^2 + y^2 = r^2$, and so the equation of the upper semi-circle is $y = \sqrt{r^2 - x^2}$. The semi-circle cuts the x axis at $-r$ and r and so the area is obtained as follows:

$$\int_{-r}^{r} y\,dx = \int_{-r}^{r} \sqrt{r^2 - x^2}\,dx$$

Substitute $x = r\sin\theta$ and $\dfrac{dx}{d\theta} = r\cos\theta$

$$= \int_{-\frac{\pi}{2}}^{\frac{\pi}{2}} \sqrt{r^2 - r^2\sin^2\theta}\; r\cos\theta\,d\theta$$

$x = r \Rightarrow \theta = \dfrac{\pi}{2}$ *and* $x = -r \Rightarrow \theta = -\dfrac{\pi}{2}$

$$= \int_{-\frac{\pi}{2}}^{\frac{\pi}{2}} r^2\cos^2\theta\,d\theta$$

$$= \tfrac{1}{2}r^2 \int_{-\frac{\pi}{2}}^{\frac{\pi}{2}} (1 + \cos 2\theta)\,d\theta$$

$\cos 2\theta = 2\cos^2\theta - 1$

$$= \tfrac{1}{2}r^2 [\theta + \tfrac{1}{2}\sin 2\theta]_{-\frac{\pi}{2}}^{\frac{\pi}{2}}$$

$\Rightarrow \cos^2\theta = \tfrac{1}{2}(1 + \cos 2\theta)$

$$= \tfrac{1}{2}\pi r^2.$$

Thus the area of a semi-circle is $\tfrac{1}{2}\pi r^2$ and, hence, the area of a circle is πr^2.

The volume obtained by rotating the area under the curve $y = f(x)$ by 2π about the x axis is given by the formula $\int \pi y^2 dx$ between suitable limits. Rotating a semi-circle of radius r by 2π about the x axis will give a sphere of radius r. The semi-circle has equation $y = \sqrt{r^2 - x^2}$ and the limits of the integral are $-r$ and r giving:

$$\text{Volume} = \int_{-r}^{r} \pi(r^2 - x^2)\,dx$$

$$= \pi[r^2 x - \tfrac{1}{3}x^3]_{-r}^{r}$$

$$= \pi(r^3 - \tfrac{1}{3}r^3 + r^3 - \tfrac{1}{3}r^3)$$

$$= \tfrac{4}{3}\pi r^3.$$

Thus, the volume of the sphere is $\tfrac{4}{3}\pi r^3$. The integration involved, perhaps surprisingly, is notably simpler than for the area of a circle.

Area and Perimeter

You may have noticed that there seems to be a connection between the area and perimeter (or circumference) of a circle. Differentiating the area formula with respect to the radius gives the formula for the perimeter.

$$P = 2\pi r \text{ and } A = \pi r^2, \quad \frac{dA}{dr} = 2\pi r = P.$$

This can be explained by noting that a small increase in the radius, δr, leads to a small increase in area given by $\delta A \approx 2\pi r \delta r$, taking the area of a narrow ring as the circumference multiplied by the width δr.

You might wonder whether a similar result holds for regular polygons.

Consider a square with edges of length l:

$$P = 4l \text{ and } A = l^2, \quad \frac{dA}{dl} = 2l \neq P.$$

The result for the derivative is similar in form, but not identical. However, the formula for the circle uses the radius, whereas that for the square uses the length of the side. So the relationship may hold for a suitably defined 'radius'.

Consider the 'radius' r of a square as the distance from the centre to a vertex. Then the length of a side is $r\sqrt{2}$.

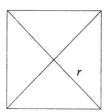

$$P = 4r\sqrt{2} \text{ and } A = 2r^2, \quad \frac{dA}{dr} = 4r \neq P.$$

Alternatively, the radius can be defined as the perpendicular distance from the centre to one of the sides. Then the length of a side is $2r$.

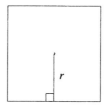

$$P = 8r \text{ and } A = 4r^2, \quad \frac{dA}{dr} = 8r = P.$$

So, with a suitably defined radius, the relationship does hold for a square. Is it valid for all regular polygons?

Consider now a regular polygon with n sides. When the ends of a side are joined to the centre of the polygon, an isosceles triangle like triangle AOB below is formed. OM is the perpendicular to AB and is defined as the 'radius' r of the polygon.

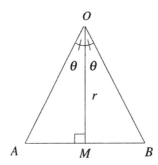

The angle AOB is equal to $\dfrac{2\pi}{n}$ and, since OM bisects the angle, angles AOM and BOM are each $\dfrac{\pi}{n}$. Then, $AM = r\tan\dfrac{\pi}{n}$ and so $AB = 2r\tan\dfrac{\pi}{n}$. It then follows that:

$$P = 2nr\tan\frac{\pi}{n} \text{ and } A = nr^2\tan\frac{\pi}{n} \quad\Rightarrow\quad \frac{dA}{dr} = 2nr\tan\frac{\pi}{n} = P.$$

So the relationship between area and perimeter is true for all regular polygons when 'radius' is defined as the perpendicular distance from the centre to a side.

One consequence of this relationship is that the formulae for area and circumference of a circle can be obtained as the limiting case when the number of sides tends to infinity!

To show this, you need to use the fact that $\dfrac{\tan\theta}{\theta} \to 1$ as $\theta \to 0$. This is explained by referring to the diagram below and considering the area of the triangle sandwiched between the areas of the two sectors .

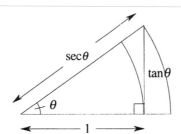

$$\frac{1}{2}\theta < \frac{1}{2}\tan\theta < \frac{1}{2}\theta\sec^2\theta \quad\Rightarrow\quad 1 < \frac{\tan\theta}{\theta} < \sec^2\theta.$$

Since $\sec^2\theta \to 1$ as $\theta \to 0$, $\dfrac{\tan\theta}{\theta} \to 1$ as $\theta \to 0$.

With $\theta = \dfrac{\pi}{n}$, $n = \dfrac{\pi}{\theta}$ and $\theta \to 0$ as $n \to \infty$. The formulae for perimeter and area of a regular polygon are expressed in terms of θ and then the behaviour as $\theta \to 0$ gives the corresponding formulae for the circle.

$$P = 2nr\tan\theta = 2\pi r\frac{\tan\theta}{\theta} \to 2\pi r \text{ as } n \to \infty.$$

$$A = nr^2\tan\theta = \pi r^2\frac{\tan\theta}{\theta} \to \pi r^2 \text{ as } n \to \infty.$$

The Central Derivative

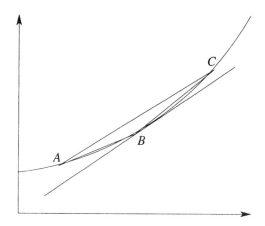

When discussing differentiation, some textbooks show a diagram which suggests that the *right derivative*, which is defined as the limit of the gradient of the chord BC in the diagram above as the point C approaches the point B. This is expressed as

$$f'(x) = \lim_{h \to 0+} \left(\frac{f(x+h) - f(x)}{h} \right),$$

where B is a general point $(x, f(x))$ and C is the point $(x+h, f(x+h))$. C is to the right of B so h has a positive value in this case, which tends towards zero as C moves towards B.

For a point A to the left of B, h as defined above becomes negative. Then the definition of the *left derivative* is

$$f'(x) = \lim_{h \to 0+} \left(\frac{f(x-h) - f(x)}{-h} \right) = \lim_{h \to 0+} \left(\frac{f(x) - f(x-h)}{h} \right).$$

This gives the limit of the gradient of the chord AB as the point A on the left approaches the point B. In what follows comments about the right derivative apply equally to the left derivative.

The *central derivative* is the limit of the gradient of the chord AC as the points A and C together move closer to the point B from left and right, corresponding again to the increment h tending to zero. Expressed algebraically this gives

$$f'(x) = \lim_{h \to 0} \left(\frac{f(x+h) - f(x-h)}{2h} \right).$$

This expression is the mean of the left and right derivatives if they both exist.

For most elementary functions, the chord AC has a gradient which is a much better approximation, for a given increment h, to the gradient of the tangent at B than the gradients of either AB or BC. This is useful in generating numerical results from which to conjecture the gradient of the tangent and leads to more elegant arguments when differentiating from first principles, if the slightly more complicated initial form is accepted. The conditions for the existence of the derivative are awkward for the central derivative. Difficulties arise, for example, at the origin in the case of $f(x) = |x|$, where the central derivative leads to an apparent value of zero when the derivative does not in fact exist. However, with simple functions, when the derivative clearly does exist it can often be found more neatly using the central derivative.

The function $f(x) = x^3$ is differentiated from first principles here to compare the two approaches.

Using the right derivative:

$$f(x) = x^3$$

$$f'(x) = \lim_{h \to 0+}\left(\frac{f(x+h) - f(x)}{h} \right)$$

$$= \lim_{h \to 0+}\left(\frac{(x+h)^3 - x^3}{h} \right)$$

$$= \lim_{h \to 0+}\left(\frac{3x^2 h + 3xh^2 + h^3}{h} \right)$$

$$= \lim_{h \to 0+}\left(3x^2 + 3xh + h^2 \right)$$

$$= 3x^2.$$

Using the central derivative:

$$f(x) = x^3$$

$$f'(x) = \lim_{h \to 0}\left(\frac{f(x+h) - f(x-h)}{2h} \right)$$

$$= \lim_{h \to 0}\left(\frac{(x+h)^3 - (x-h)^3}{2h} \right)$$

$$= \lim_{h \to 0}\left(\frac{6x^2 h + 2h^3}{2h} \right)$$

$$= \lim_{h \to 0}\left(3x^2 + h^2 \right)$$

$$= 3x^2.$$

So far there might seem to be little gain, although it should be clear from this why you get closer approximations when working numerically.

The example of $f(x) = \sin x$ is more telling.

Both approaches in this case require familiarity with the following two results, which are stated here without proof:

$$\sin(\theta + \phi) - \sin(\theta - \phi) = 2\cos\theta\sin\phi.$$

$$\lim_{h \to 0}\left(\frac{\sin h}{h} \right) = 1, \text{ where } h \text{ is measured in radians.}$$

Using the right derivative:

$$f(x) = \sin x$$

$$f'(x) = \lim_{h \to 0+}\left(\frac{f(x+h) - f(x)}{h}\right)$$

$$= \lim_{h \to 0+}\left(\frac{\sin(x+h) - \sin x}{h}\right)$$

$$= \lim_{h \to 0+}\left(\frac{\sin((x+\frac{1}{2}h)+\frac{1}{2}h) - \sin((x+\frac{1}{2}h)-\frac{1}{2}h)}{h}\right)$$

$$= \lim_{h \to 0+}\left(\frac{2\cos(x+\frac{1}{2}h)\sin\frac{1}{2}h}{h}\right)$$

$$= \lim_{h \to 0+}\left(\cos(x+\tfrac{1}{2}h)\right)\lim_{h \to 0}\left(\frac{\sin\frac{1}{2}h}{\frac{1}{2}h}\right)$$

$$= \cos x.$$

Using the central derivative:

$$f(x) = \sin x$$

$$f'(x) = \lim_{h \to 0}\left(\frac{f(x+h) - f(x-h)}{2h}\right)$$

$$= \lim_{h \to 0}\left(\frac{\sin(x+h) - \sin(x-h)}{2h}\right)$$

$$= \lim_{h \to 0}\left(\frac{2\cos x\sin h}{2h}\right)$$

$$= \cos x\lim_{h \to 0}\left(\frac{\sin h}{h}\right)$$

$$= \cos x.$$

Not only is the simplification more straightforward here, but you only have to deal with the limit of $\dfrac{\sin h}{h}$ as h tends to zero.

5.3 Try This

Use the central derivative to find $f'(x)$ from first principles for:

$$f(x) = x^2 \qquad f(x) = x^4 \qquad f(x) = \frac{1}{x} \text{ for } x \neq 0 \qquad f(x) = \cos x$$

Chapter Six

Are You Sure?

Dissecting a Circle

$n = 1$
$R = 1$

$n = 2$
$R = 2$

$n = 3$
$R = 4$

$n = 4$
$R = 8$

$n = 5$
$R = 16$

Each point (or node) on the circle is joined to every other point. The points are arranged so that no inside point is the intersection of more than two lines.

6.1 Try This

How many regions when $n = 6$?

Try drawing a picture.

How does R seem to be related to n?

How many regions would this give for $n = 11$?

Does your answer seem plausible?

Euler's Formula for a connected network on the surface of a sphere states that $N - A + R = 2$, where N is the number of nodes (or vertices), A is the number of arcs (or edges) and R is the number of regions (or faces). This is equivalent to the result for polyhedra: $V - E + F = 2$ (see chapter 2). The formula becomes $N - A + R = 1$ for a network on a plane, if the outside region, which corresponds to one region on a sphere, is not counted.

Using Euler's Formula we can deduce the relationship between R and n.

Firstly, consider the number of nodes.

There are n boundary points. Each set of 4 boundary points contributes one inside point (compare the case where $n = 4$). So, the number of inside points is $^nC_4$.

It follows that:

$$\text{Total number of nodes} = {}^nC_4 + n$$

Secondly, consider the number of arcs.

Each boundary point lies on $n+1$ arcs: the $n-1$ diagonals from that point plus 2 adjacent arcs on the boundary. Since there are n boundary points, this gives $n(n+1)$ arcs.

Each inside point lies on 4 arcs. This gives $4\,{}^nC_4$ arcs.

Since each arc has a point at each end:

$$\text{Total number of arcs} = \tfrac{1}{2}(4\,{}^nC_4 + n(n+1))$$
$$= 2\,{}^nC_4 + \tfrac{1}{2}n(n+1).$$

Using Euler's Formula:

$$\text{Number of regions, } R = A - N + 1$$
$$= 2\,{}^nC_4 + \tfrac{1}{2}n(n+1) - {}^nC_4 - n + 1$$
$$= {}^nC_4 + \tfrac{1}{2}n(n-1) + 1$$
$$= {}^nC_4 + {}^nC_2 + 1, \quad \text{since } {}^nC_2 = \tfrac{1}{2}n(n-1).$$

Note that this can be written as $\binom{n}{4} + \binom{n}{2} + 1$ using the alternative notation.

The formula gives values as follows:

n	${}^nC_4 + {}^nC_2 + 1$
1	1
2	2
3	4
4	8
5	16
6	31

So, you see it is not 32 after all - you did not make a mistake when counting!

6.2 Try This

How many regions are there when $n = 11$?

All Triangles are Equilateral

Consider this 'proof' that all triangles are equilateral. First we prove that all triangles are isosceles. Your challenge is to spot what is wrong with the 'proof'.

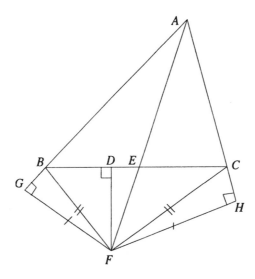

In the diagram, *ABC* is a general triangle.

AE bisects angle *A* and *DF* is the perpendicular bisector of *BC* meeting *AE* produced at *F*.

It follows that triangle *BCF* is isosceles, and so *BF = FC*.

FG and *FH* are perpendiculars from *F* to the sides *AB* and *AC* produced. Since *AF* is the angle bisector, *FG = FH*.

So, *AFH* is congruent to *AFG*, since *AF* is common to both triangles, *FG = FH* and all the angles are the same. Hence, *AG = AH*.

Triangle *BFG* is congruent to triangle *CFH*, since *BF = CF*, *FG = FH* and the angles at *G* and *H* are right angles. Hence, *BG = CH*.

Now, *AB = AG – BG* and *AC = AH – CH* and, therefore, *AB = AC*.

This means that triangle *ABC* is isosceles.

Applying the same argument to another pair of sides, it follows that all triangles are equilateral.

6.3 Try This

Where is the error?

Try drawing the diagram for yourself.

Can you put points *G* and *H* as they are in the diagram?

Surprising Results

Besides the previous example, the first page of chapter 2 highlighted the dangers of arguing from plausible-looking pictures. These two arguments show the dangers of this when limits are involved as well.

$\sqrt{2} = 2$?

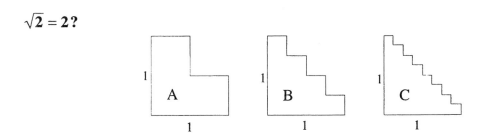

Diagram A has 2 steps. The length and width of each step is $\frac{1}{2}$.
So, the total distance covered by the steps is $4 \times \frac{1}{2} = 2$.

Diagram B has 4 steps and again the total distance is $8 \times \frac{1}{4} = 2$.

Diagram C has 8 steps and again the total distance is $16 \times \frac{1}{8} = 2$.

So, for n steps the distance covered is $2n \times \dfrac{1}{n} = 2$.

The limit of the step diagram appears to be a right-angled isosceles triangle with a hypotenuse whose length is $\sqrt{2}$.

The argument seems to show that $\sqrt{2} = 2$, but, in fact, the limit of the staircase as the number of stairs increases is not a straight line even though it may look like it.

$\pi = 2$?

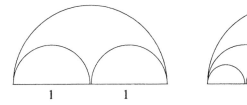

In the first diagram, the large semi-circle has unit radius and arc length π. The smaller semi-circle has arc length $\dfrac{\pi}{2}$ and so the total length is π.

In the second diagram, the smallest semi-circles have arc length $\dfrac{\pi}{4}$, so again the total arc length is π. Carrying on this process, the total arc length is always π, but the limiting case is a straight line of length 2. The argument appears to show that $\pi = 2$.

Seemingly simple situations involving numbers can also produce strange and surprising results. These three final examples further illustrate the difficulties involved in dealing with the infinite.

Summing a Series

Consider the sum of the series $S = 1 - 1 + 1 - 1 + 1 - 1 + ...$

a) Grouping the terms:

$$S = (1 - 1) + (1 - 1) + (1 - 1) + ...$$
$$= 0 + 0 + 0 + ...$$
$$= 0.$$

b) Grouping the terms differently:

$$S = 1 + (-1 + 1) + (-1 + 1) + (-1 + 1) + ...$$
$$= 1 + 0 + 0 + 0 + ...$$
$$= 1$$

c) Grouping the terms in another way:

$$S = 1 + (-1 + 1) + (-1 + 1) + (-1 + 1) + ...$$
$$= 1 + (1 + -1) + (1 + -1) + (1 + -1) + ...$$
$$= 1 + 1 + (-1 + 1) + (-1 + 1) + (-1 + 1) + ...$$
$$= 1 + 1 + 0 + 0 + 0 + ...$$
$$= 2.$$

It is clear that the infinite series does not converge – there is no sum to infinity. The example points to the dangers that apparently reasonable rearrangements of brackets can cause if they are extended to an infinite number of terms. It also serves to remind us of what goes wrong if we ignore the fact that a geometric series only converges when $|r| < 1$, where r is the common ratio.

6.4 Try This

Try finding some false values for the sum of this series:

$$S = 1 - 2 + 4 - 8 + 16 - 32 + ...$$

70

Counting Natural Numbers

N is the set of natural numbers: $\mathbf{N} = \{0, 1, 2, 3, \dots\}$ and **E** is the set of even numbers: $\mathbf{E} = \{0, 2, 4, 6, \dots\}$.

E is a subset of **N**, but the sets are not equal, since **N** contains all the odd numbers. Therefore you would expect **N** to be a bigger set than **E**.

The function f defined by $f(n) = 2n$ maps **N** onto **E** as shown below:

0	1	2	3	4	5		N
⇕	⇕	⇕	⇕	⇕	⇕	...	
0	2	4	6	8	10		E

Continuing the pairings suggests that the sets **N** and **E** are the same size, which is contrary to our intuition, but is apparently true.

Mapping an Interval

R is the set of real numbers and $(0, 1) = \{x \in \mathbf{R} : 0 < x < 1\}$ is the set of all the real numbers in the interval between 0 and 1 exclusive.

Now $(0, 1)$ is clearly a subset of **R**, and $(0, 1)$ should be smaller than **R**.

$(0, 1)$ can be mapped onto $\left(-\dfrac{\pi}{2}, \dfrac{\pi}{2}\right)$ by the function $x \to \pi x - \dfrac{\pi}{2}$. Then the function $x \to \tan x$ maps the interval $\left(-\dfrac{\pi}{2}, \dfrac{\pi}{2}\right)$ onto **R**. Thus for all $y \in \mathbf{R}$, there is an $x \in \left(-\dfrac{\pi}{2}, \dfrac{\pi}{2}\right)$ such that $y = \tan x$.

So, using composition of functions, $x \to \tan(\pi x - \dfrac{\pi}{2})$ maps $(0, 1)$ onto **R**. The graph of $y = \tan(\pi x - \dfrac{\pi}{2})$ shown below illustrates this.

Every number in **R** is the image of some number in $(0, 1)$. So, in fact, $(0, 1)$ is at least as great as **R**!

Intuition or Proof?

The first example in this chapter brings out very effectively the dangers of plausible patterns. Patterns are valuable as a way of suggesting conjectures, but what seems to be so obvious may not be right, and a single counterexample is sufficient to show this. Many mathematical results are valid for infinitely many cases, so that no amount of checking of individual cases can be sufficient to provide a proof – arguments have to take a different general form.

All triangles are obviously not equilateral and the spurious proof illustrates the dangers of reasoning from plausible-looking diagrams. The conclusion is obviously wrong in this case, so it is clear that there must be something wrong with the proof. However, when a result seems to be obviously true, it is just as vital to check for faulty assumptions or incorrect reasoning in an attempted proof.

The results concerning the values of $\sqrt{2}$ and π are again obviously not true, but the two examples illustrate well the inherent difficulties involved in limiting processes. They point to the need for caution in accepting arguments like the one in chapter 5 which claims to prove the formula for the area of a circle, and more widely to all the limiting arguments that underpin the calculus.

The fact that summing a series in different, seemingly legitimate, ways leads to different answers illustrates the problems of the infinite in a different way. You cannot necessarily assume that procedures which are valid for a finite number of terms will still be correct when there are infinitely many terms.

The final examples, on the other hand, give results which, like $0.\dot{9} = 1$ at the start of chapter 1, seem to defy common sense, but they are in fact true! Intuition is not always a good guide to the truth of conjectures in mathematics. Intuition can lead to wrong ideas, but, on the other hand, something that seems to be very unlikely can turn out to be true. This only serves to emphasise the crucial need for clear and rigorous thinking and provides one of the key reasons why proof is so important and why mathematics is such a perpetual source of fascination.

Commentary

Page 1

It certainly seems intuitively obvious that you cannot find a number that lies between $0.\dot{9}$ and 1, but it is not so easy to prove this satisfactorily in a way that is sufficiently elementary for use at school level.

Although the argument from pattern in method 2 seems plausible, it does depend on accepting that $\frac{1}{9} = 0.\dot{1}$ and that raises essentially the same issues as those involved in accepting that $1 = 0.\dot{9}$.

Method 3 is dependent on accepting the validity of the operations carried out on a recurring decimal. Is it valid to multiply by 10 and carry out a subtraction in this way? In fact the argument is valid, but some of the examples in Chapter 6 show the need for extreme caution in operating with infinite series as we are here.

The geometric series approach of method 4 is essentially the same as method 3, since a proof of the formula for the sum is usually obtained using a generalisation of that approach.

An interesting discussion of the difficulties underlying the result that $0.\dot{9} = 1$ will be found in an interesting article by Bob Burn in the March 1997 issue of the Mathematical Gazette.

Page 7, 2.1

The square has an area of 64 and the rectangle has an area of 65, so where has the extra area come from? The interesting question here is to explain what has gone wrong! The gradient of the diagonal of the rectangle is $\frac{5}{13}$, whereas the gradient of the hypotenuse of the triangle is $\frac{3}{8}$. Since $\frac{5}{13} \neq \frac{3}{8}$, the hypotenuse and the diagonal are not the same straight line. Using tangents you can verify that the angles of slope are approximately $20.6°$ and $21.0°$ respectively. Your eye is unlikely to detect this difference of about $0.4°$!

Page 10, 2.2

Using angle properties of parallel lines it then follows that:

$$f = b \qquad \textit{alternate angles}$$
$$g = c \qquad \textit{alternate angles}$$
$$a + f + g = 180 \qquad \textit{angles on a straight line.}$$

Hence, $a + b + c = 180$ and so the angles of a triangle add up to $180°$.

Page 19, 2.4, Question 1

Area of kite $BEOF = 2 \times$ area of triangle $BEO = 2 \times \dfrac{1}{2} OE \times BE = r(a - r)$.

Page 19, 2.4, Question 2

$AD = AF$ and $BE = BF$ because the distances along the two tangents from a point outside a circle to that circle are equal.

Page 19, 2.4, Question 3

$c = BA = BF + AF = BE + AD = (a - r) + (b - r) = a + b - 2r.$

Page 19, 2.4, Question 4

$c^2 = ((a + b) - 2r)^2 = (a + b)^2 - 4r(a + b) + 4r^2.$

Page 19, 2.4, Question 5

Since $ab = 2ar + 2br - 2r^2$, it follows that $2ab - 4(ar + br - r^2) = 2ab - 4 \times \frac{1}{2}ab = 0.$

Page 24, 2.5, Question 1

Let $y = \cos^2 \theta + \sin^2 \theta.$

Then, $\dfrac{d}{d\theta}(\cos^2 \theta) = -2\sin \theta \cos \theta$ and $\dfrac{d}{d\theta}(\sin^2 \theta) = 2\sin \theta \cos \theta.$

Hence, $\dfrac{d}{d\theta}(\cos^2 \theta + \sin^2 \theta) = -2\sin \theta \cos \theta + 2\sin \theta \cos \theta = 0.$

Since $\dfrac{dy}{d\theta} = 0$, y is a constant.

Only one value of θ is needed to find the constant. $\theta = 0$ is one value to use, but any value of θ will do.

When $\theta = 0$, $y = \cos^2 0 + \sin^2 0 = 1$, and so $\cos^2 \theta + \sin^2 \theta = 1$ for all values of θ.

Page 24, 2.5, Question 2

A rotation through an angle θ is represented by the matrix $\mathbf{R}_\theta = \begin{bmatrix} \cos \theta & -\sin \theta \\ \sin \theta & \cos \theta \end{bmatrix}.$

Since a rotation does not alter the area of a shape this means that $\det \mathbf{R}_\theta = 1.$

$\det \mathbf{R}_\theta = \cos \theta \cos \theta - (-\sin \theta)\sin \theta = \cos^2 \theta + \sin^2 \theta$, and so $\cos^2 \theta + \sin^2 \theta = 1.$

Page 24, 2.5, Question 3

A rotation through an angle θ followed by another rotation through an angle $-\theta$ returns the shape to its original position. Combining the two matrices gives the identity matrix.

$$\mathbf{R}_\theta = \begin{bmatrix} \cos\theta & -\sin\theta \\ \sin\theta & \cos\theta \end{bmatrix} \text{ and } \mathbf{R}_{-\theta} = \begin{bmatrix} \cos(-\theta) & -\sin(-\theta) \\ \sin(-\theta) & \cos(-\theta) \end{bmatrix} = \begin{bmatrix} \cos\theta & \sin\theta \\ -\sin\theta & \cos\theta \end{bmatrix}.$$

$$\mathbf{R}_\theta\mathbf{R}_{-\theta} = \begin{bmatrix} \cos\theta & -\sin\theta \\ \sin\theta & \cos\theta \end{bmatrix}\begin{bmatrix} \cos\theta & \sin\theta \\ -\sin\theta & \cos\theta \end{bmatrix} = \begin{bmatrix} \cos^2\theta + \sin^2\theta & 0 \\ 0 & \cos^2\theta + \sin^2\theta \end{bmatrix}.$$

Since $\mathbf{R}_\theta\mathbf{R}_{-\theta} = \mathbf{I} = \begin{bmatrix} 1 & 0 \\ 0 & 1 \end{bmatrix}$, it follows that $\cos^2\theta + \sin^2\theta = 1$. Note that $\mathbf{R}_{-\theta}\mathbf{R}_\theta = \mathbf{I}$ also.

Page 24, 2.5, Question 4

$$\cos^2\theta = \left(1 - \frac{\theta^2}{2!} + \frac{\theta^4}{4!} - \frac{\theta^6}{6!} + \dots\right)^2 \qquad \sin^2\theta = \left(\theta - \frac{\theta^3}{3!} + \frac{\theta^5}{5!} - \frac{\theta^7}{7!} + \dots\right)^2$$

$$= 1 - \theta^2 + \frac{\theta^4}{3} - \frac{2\theta^6}{45} + \dots \qquad\qquad = \theta^2 - \frac{\theta^4}{3} + \frac{2\theta^6}{45} - \dots$$

This is a bit messy, but it does appear to show how the non-constant terms start to cancel out. However, as the examples in the final chapter suggest, there are potential difficulties in manipulating infinite series in this way. It is appropriate, therefore, to be wary about accepting arguments like this. This question, and questions 5 and 6, use results that are more advanced than the result that is being proved, but they are nonetheless instructive in showing links between different ideas.

Page 24, 2.5, Question 5

Since $e^{i\theta} = \cos\theta + i\sin\theta$, $e^{-i\theta} = \cos(-\theta) + i\sin(-\theta) = \cos\theta - i\sin\theta$.

So, $e^{i\theta}e^{-i\theta} = (\cos\theta + i\sin\theta)(\cos\theta - i\sin\theta) = \cos^2\theta - i^2\sin^2\theta = \cos^2\theta + \sin^2\theta$.

Since $e^{i\theta}e^{-i\theta} = e^0 = 1$, it follows that $\cos^2\theta + \sin^2\theta = 1$.

Page 24, 2.5, Question 6

$$\cos^2\theta = \left(\frac{e^{i\theta} + e^{-i\theta}}{2}\right)^2 = \frac{(e^{i\theta})^2 + 2e^{i\theta}e^{-i\theta} + (e^{-i\theta})^2}{4} = \frac{e^{2i\theta} + 2 + e^{-2i\theta}}{4}.$$

Similarly, $\sin^2\theta = \left(\frac{e^{i\theta} - e^{-i\theta}}{2i}\right)^2 = \frac{-(e^{2i\theta} - 2 + e^{-2i\theta})}{4}.$

Hence, $\cos^2\theta + \sin^2\theta = 1$.

Page 26, 2.6

In the left-hand diagram, the point on the circumference is moved so that both isosceles triangles are on the same side of the line joining the centre to the point on the circumference. In this case the angle at the circumference becomes $x - y$ (or $y - x$), and the angle at the centre is $2x - 2y$ (or $2y - 2x$).

In the right-hand diagram, it is the reflex angle at the centre that is twice the corresponding angle at the circumference. The original proof using isosceles triangles still holds.

Page 27, 2.7

$\angle QPO = \angle PQO = \theta$, because triangle OPQ is isosceles.

Then, $\angle QOR = 2\theta$, since $\angle QOP = 180 - 2\theta$.

Hence, $\angle QRO = \angle RQO = \frac{1}{2}(180 - 2\theta) = 90 - \theta$, because triangle ORQ is isosceles.

Finally, it follows that $\angle PQR = \angle PQO + \angle RQO = \theta + (90 - \theta) = 90$.

An alternative way to look at this is to label the equal pairs of angles in the isosceles triangle as shown.

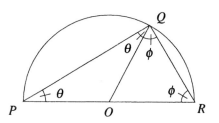

Since $\theta + \theta + \phi + \phi = 180$, using the angle sum of triangle PQR, it then follows that $\angle PQR = \theta + \phi = 90$.

Page 28, 2.8, Question 1

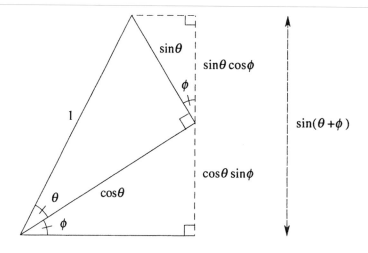

$$\sin(\theta + \phi) = \sin\theta \cos\phi + \cos\theta \sin\phi.$$

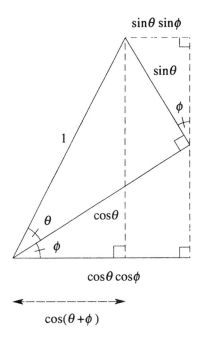

$$\cos(\theta + \phi) = \cos\theta\cos\phi - \sin\theta\sin\phi.$$

Note that these proofs only work when $\theta > 0$ and $\phi > 0$ and $\theta + \phi < 90$. They are a first step in proving the formulae for all θ and ϕ.

Page 28, 2.8, Question 2

$\angle PQR$ is a right angle, since it is an angle in a semi-circle.

If $\angle QOR = \alpha$ then $\angle POQ = 180 - \alpha$ and $\angle QPO = \dfrac{\alpha}{2}$ as triangle OPQ is isosceles.

So $\angle PRQ = 90 - \dfrac{\alpha}{2}$ and hence $\angle SQR = \dfrac{\alpha}{2}$.

In triangle OQS, $OS = \cos\alpha$ and $QS = \sin\alpha$.

Thus, in triangle PQS, $\tan\dfrac{\alpha}{2} = \dfrac{\sin\alpha}{1 + \cos\alpha}$, and in triangle QRS, $\tan\dfrac{\alpha}{2} = \dfrac{1 - \cos\alpha}{\sin\alpha}$.

In this case, the angle α has been taken as acute. The argument can be extended to the case where α is obtuse, but it is important to note that the first formula is not valid for $\alpha = 180°$ and the second for $\alpha = 0°$.

Page 28, 2.8, Question 3

From triangle ADE, $\tan EAD = \dfrac{1}{2}$. From triangle ACD, $\tan CAB = \dfrac{1}{3}$.

By Pythagoras, $AE = EB = \sqrt{5}$ and $AB = \sqrt{10}$, and so $AE^2 + EB^2 = AB^2$.

Hence, by the converse of Pythagoras' Theorem, triangle EAB is an isosceles right-angled triangle with $\angle EAB = 45°$.

Since $\angle EAD + \angle CAB = \angle EAB$, it follows that $\tan^{-1}\dfrac{1}{2} + \tan^{-1}\dfrac{1}{3} = 45°$.

The usual algebraic proof of this result uses $\tan(A+B) = \dfrac{\tan A + \tan B}{1 - \tan A \tan B}$, setting $A = \tan^{-1}\dfrac{1}{2}$ and $B = \tan^{-1}\dfrac{1}{3}$ to give $\dfrac{\frac{1}{2} + \frac{1}{3}}{1 - \frac{1}{2} \times \frac{1}{3}} = 1 = \tan 45°$.

The diagram below (in which the grid square side is 2 units) demonstrates the result $\tan^{-1}\dfrac{1}{3} = \tan^{-1}\dfrac{1}{5} + \tan^{-1}\dfrac{1}{8}$.

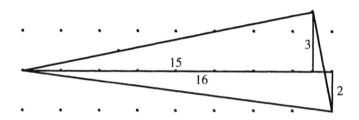

The presence of numbers from the Fibonacci sequence here is not a coincidence. A proof of the following general result is left as a challenge for you!

$$\tan^{-1}\frac{1}{F_{2n}} = \tan^{-1}\frac{1}{F_{2n+1}} + \tan^{-1}\frac{1}{F_{2n+2}}.$$

Page 30, 2.9

Any point on the median CR, where R is the midpoint of AB, can be written as $\mathbf{c} + v(\frac{1}{2}\mathbf{b} - \mathbf{c})$, since $\overrightarrow{CR} = \frac{1}{2}\mathbf{b} - \mathbf{c}$. Putting $v = \frac{2}{3}$ gives the point $\frac{1}{3}(\mathbf{b} + \mathbf{c})$, showing that CR passes through the point of intersection of the other pair of medians and is also divided in the ratio 2:1.

Page 32, 3.1

$$
\begin{aligned}
2 \times {}^{-}3 &= 2 \times {}^{-}3 + 0 \\
&= 2 \times {}^{-}3 + {}^{-}2 \times({}^{-}3 + 3) \\
&= 2 \times {}^{-}3 + ({}^{-}2 \times {}^{-}3 + {}^{-}2 \times 3) \\
&= (2 \times {}^{-}3 + {}^{-}2 \times {}^{-}3) + {}^{-}2 \times 3 \\
&= (2 + {}^{-}2) \times {}^{-}3 + {}^{-}2 \times 3 \\
&= 0 + {}^{-}2 \times 3 \\
&= {}^{-}2 \times 3.
\end{aligned}
$$

Page 34, 3.3

The four consecutive numbers may be denoted by $n, n+1, n+2, n+3$.

- The difference between the product of the second and fourth and the product of the first and third is the sum of the middle pair of terms (or the outer pair).

$$\begin{aligned} \text{Difference of products} &= (n+1)(n+3) - n(n+2) \\ &= (n^2 + 4n + 3) - (n^2 + 2n) \\ &= 2n + 3. \\ \text{Sum of middle pair} &= (n+1) + (n+2) \\ &= 2n + 3. \end{aligned}$$

- The difference between the product of the second and third and the product of the first and fourth is 2.

$$(n+1)(n+2) - n(n+3) = (n^2 + 3n + 2) - (n^2 + 3n) = 2.$$

Here are two results using three consecutive numbers. It is convenient in this case to denote the three numbers by $n-1, n$ and $n+1$.

- The product of the outer pair is one less than the square of the middle number.

$$\text{Product of outer pair} = (n-1)(n+1) = n^2 - 1.$$

- The product of the first and second pair differ by twice the middle number.

$$n(n+1) - n(n-1) = (n^2 + n) - (n^2 - n) = 2n .$$

In the case of five consecutive numbers the numbers are conveniently referred to as $n-2, n-1, n, n+1$ and $n+2$. Four results are given below.

- The product of the outer pair is four less than the square of the middle number.

$$\text{Product of outer pair} = (n-2)(n+2) = n^2 - 4.$$

- The difference between the product of the first pair and the product of the last pair is six times the middle number.

$$(n+1)(n+2) - (n-1)(n-2) = (n^2 + 3n + 2) - (n^2 - 3n + 2) = 6n .$$

- The difference between the product of the second and fourth numbers and the product of the first and fifth numbers is 3.

$$(n-1)(n+1) - (n-2)(n+2) = (n^2 - 1) - (n^2 - 4) = 3 .$$

- The difference between the product of the second and fifth numbers and the product of the first and fourth numbers is twice the middle number.

$$(n-1)(n+2) - (n+1)(n-2) = (n^2 + n - 2) - (n^2 - n - 2) = 2n .$$

Page 35, 3.4

The first six numbers of the form Q are:

$$2 + 1 = 3$$
$$2 \times 3 + 1 = 7$$
$$2 \times 3 \times 5 + 1 = 31$$
$$2 \times 3 \times 5 \times 7 + 1 = 211$$
$$2 \times 3 \times 5 \times 7 \times 11 + 1 = 2311$$
$$2 \times 3 \times 5 \times 7 \times 11 \times 13 + 1 = 30031.$$

The first five are prime, but the sixth is not, since $30031 = 59 \times 509$ and we note, as required by the proof, that its factors are bigger than 13, the largest prime used in its construction.

Page 36, 3.5

All odd numbers are of the form $4n \pm 1$ and so all prime numbers, except 2, are of this form. Obviously, as with $6n \pm 1$, the converse is not true.

Page 37, 3.6

There are four cases to consider here. In the first case, we consider primes that are both immediately above a multiple of 6.

$$(6m + 1)^2 - (6n + 1)^2 = (6(m + n) + 2)6(m - n)$$
$$= 12(3(m + n) + 1)(m - n).$$

Either m and n are of the same parity (both even or both odd) so that $m - n$ is even,

or m and n are of opposite parity (one even and one odd) so that $3(m + n) + 1$ is even.

For either case it follows that $12(3(m + n) + 1)(m - n)$ is a multiple of 24.

The other three cases to consider are

$$(6m - 1)^2 - (6n - 1)^2, \quad (6m + 1)^2 - (6n - 1)^2 \quad \text{and} \quad (6m - 1)^2 - (6n + 1)^2.$$

The arguments are similar and the details are left to the reader.

Page 38, 3.7

When we test intuitively to see if a number is even, we simply look at the units digit, because all multiples of 10 are divisible by 2.

In the same way, looking at the last three digits is sufficient to test for divisibility by 8, since 1000 is divisible by 8. This generalises readily to testing for divisibility by higher powers of 2.

Page 39, 3.8

> To test for divisibility by 11 add both sets of alternate digits and find the difference between the two sums. A number is divisible by 11 if and only if this difference is divisible by 11.

For example, 8384629 gives $3+4+2=9$ and $8+8+6+9=31$. Since $31-9=22$ and 22 is divisible by 11, it follows that 8384629 is also divisible by 11.

Here is a simple proof for the case of a 3-digit number.

A number with digits a, b and c can be expressed as $100a+10b+c$.

Since $100a+10b+c=99a+11b+a-b+c$, it follows that $100a+10b+c$ is divisible by 11 if and only if $a-b+c$ is divisible by 11.

A general proof for a number with any number of digits can then be constructed.

A number with digits $a_n, a_{n-1}, \ldots, a_1, a_0$ can be expressed as

$$N = 10^n a_n + 10^{n-1} a_{n-1} \ldots \ldots 10a_1 + a_0.$$

The binomial theorem gives

$$10^n = (11-1)^n = 11^n - {}^nC_1 11^{n-1} + {}^nC_2 11^{n-2} - \ldots + (-1)^n = 11p + (-1)^n,$$

where p is an integer. It then follows, with q as another integer, that

$$N = 11q + (-1)^n a_n + (-1)^{n-1} a_{n-1} + \ldots + (-1)a_1 + a_0,$$

Since the signs of the powers of -1 alternate, N is divisible by 11 if and only if $a_0 - a_1 + a_2 - a_3 + a_4 - a_5 + \ldots$ is divisible by 11.

Page 41, 3.9

Proof 1 for $\sqrt{3}$

Suppose that $\sqrt{3} = \dfrac{p}{q}$, where p and q are positive integers with no common factor.

Then, $p^2 = 3q^2$ which implies that p^2 is a multiple of 3, and therefore that p is also a multiple of 3.

So, let $p = 3r$ giving $9r^2 = 3q^2$.

This gives $q^2 = 3r^2$, which implies that q^2, and therefore q, is also a multiple of 3. Since p and q cannot both be multiples of 3 the original assumption must be false.

Proof 2 for $\sqrt{3}$

As in proof 1, suppose that $\sqrt{3} = \dfrac{p}{q}$, where p and q are positive integers with no common factor. As before, $p^2 = 3q^2$.

Now p^2, as a square number, has an *even* number of prime factors, but $3q^2$ has an *odd* number of prime factors, which is a contradiction. So the original assumption is false.

Proof 1 for $\sqrt[3]{2}$

Suppose that $\sqrt[3]{2} = \dfrac{p}{q}$, where p and q are positive integers with no common factor.

Then, $p^3 = 2q^3$ which implies that p is even. So let $p = 2r$ giving $8r^3 = 2q^3$.

This gives $q^3 = 4r^3$, which implies that q^3, and therefore q, is also even. Since p and q cannot both be even, the original assumption must be false.

Proof 2 for $\sqrt[3]{2}$

As in proof 1, suppose that $\sqrt[3]{2} = \dfrac{p}{q}$, where p and q are positive integers with no common factor. Then $p^3 = 3q^3$.

Now the number of prime factors of p^3, as a perfect cube, is a multiple of 3, whereas the number of factors of $3q^3$ is one more than a multiple of 3, which is a contradiction. So the original assumption is false.

An attempted proof for $\sqrt{9}$

Suppose, using the method of the first proof 1 above, that $\sqrt{9} = \dfrac{p}{q}$, where p and q are positive integers with no common factor. Then $p^2 = 9q^2$, which implies that p^2 is a multiple of 9, but it does not now follow that p is also a multiple of 9, because, if p was a multiple of 3, p^2 would be a multiple of 9. The proof breaks down at this point, because there will not be a contradiction.

Page 43, 4.1

Replacing b with $\dfrac{b}{a}$ and c with $\dfrac{c}{a}$ in $x = \dfrac{-b \pm \sqrt{b^2 - 4c}}{2}$ gives:

$$x = \frac{-\dfrac{b}{a} \pm \sqrt{\left(\dfrac{b}{a}\right)^2 - 4\left(\dfrac{c}{a}\right)}}{2} = \frac{-b \pm \sqrt{b^2 - 4ac}}{2a}.$$

The expression has been simplified by multiplying the top and bottom by a.

Page 43, 4.2

Substituting $p = \dfrac{-b}{2a}$ into the equation $a(p+d)^2 + b(p+d) + c = 0$ gives:

$$a\left(d - \frac{b}{2a}\right)^2 + b\left(d - \frac{b}{2a}\right) + c = 0$$

$$ad^2 - bd + \frac{b^2}{4a} + bd - \frac{b^2}{2a} + c = 0$$

$$ad^2 = \frac{b^2}{4a} - c$$

$$d^2 = \frac{b^2 - 4ac}{4a^2}$$

$$d = \frac{\pm\sqrt{b^2 - 4ac}}{2a}.$$

Page 45, 4.3

$^nC_0 = 1$ for all values of n, since 0 items can only be chosen in one way. However, the formula gives $^nC_0 = \dfrac{n!}{n!0!} = \dfrac{1}{0!}$. It follows from this that $0! = 1$.

At first sight this seems to defy common sense, but the pattern in the sequence obtained by evaluating $n!$ for n from 5 to 1 makes it seem reasonable for 1 to be the next term.

$$120 \xrightarrow{\div 5} 24 \xrightarrow{\div 4} 6 \xrightarrow{\div 3} 2 \xrightarrow{\div 2} 1 \xrightarrow{\div 1} 1.$$

Page 49, 4.4

Suppose that $R_S < R_P$, contrary to what has to be proved,. It follows that:

$$a + b < \frac{ab}{a+b}$$

$$(a+b)^2 < ab \quad \text{(since } a \text{ and } b \text{ are positive)}$$

$$a^2 + ab + b^2 < 0.$$

Since a and b are both positive this gives a contradiction, so the initial statement is false and $R_S \geq R_P$, as required.

Page 56, 4.5, Question 1

It is certainly true for $n = 1$, since $\frac{1}{6}n(n+1)(2n+1) = 1$ when $n = 1$.

Suppose that it is true for $n = k$ and consider what happens for $n = k + 1$:

$$\sum_{i=1}^{k+1} r^2 = \frac{1}{6}k(k+1)(2k+1) + (k+1)^2$$

$$= \frac{1}{6}(k+1)(k(2k+1) + 6(k+1))$$

$$= \frac{1}{6}(k+1)(2k^2 + 7k + 6)$$

$$= \frac{1}{6}(k+1)(k+2)(2k+3)$$

$$= \frac{1}{6}(k+1)(k+2)(2(k+1)+1).$$

If the result is true for $n = k$, then it is true for $n = k + 1$. Since it is true for $n = 1$, it must then be true for all positive integer values of n.

A number of alternative pictorial proofs of this result and many others will be found in Roger Nelsen's book *Proofs without Words*.

Page 56, 4.5, Question 2

When $n = 1$, $n^3 + 2n = 3$, which is divisible by 3, so the result is true when $n = 1$.

Suppose that it is true for $n = k$, and consider the case where $n = k + 1$:

$$(k+1)^3 + 2(k+1) = k^3 + 3k^2 + 3k + 1 + 2k + 2$$

$$= k^3 + 2k + 3(k^2 + k + 1).$$

$3(k^2 + k + 1)$ is divisible by 3. If $k^3 + 2k$ is divisible by 3 then so is $(k+1)^3 + 2(k+1)$. Since the result is true for $n = 1$, it must then be true for all positive integer values of n.

Page 56, 4.5, Question 3

It is true for $n = 1$, since $F_1^2 = 1^2 = 1 \times 1 = F_1 \times F_2$.

Suppose that it is true for $n = k$: $\displaystyle\sum_{i=1}^{k} F_i^2 = F_k F_{k+1}$.

Add on the next term: $\displaystyle\sum_{i=1}^{k+1} F_i^2 = F_k F_{k+1} + F_{k+1}^2 = F_{k+1}(F_k + F_{k+1}) = F_{k+1} F_{k+2}$.

Hence, if the result is true for $n = k$, then it is true for $n = k+1$. Since it is true for $n = 1$, it is true for all positive integer values of n.

Page 56, 4.5, Question 4

It is true for $n = 1$, since $\dfrac{1}{n(n+1)} = \dfrac{1}{2}$ and $\dfrac{n}{n+1} = \dfrac{1}{2}$.

Suppose that it is true for $n = k$ and add on the next term:

$$\frac{1}{1.2} + \frac{1}{2.3} + \frac{1}{3.4} + \ldots + \frac{1}{k(k+1)} + \frac{1}{(k+1)(k+2)} = \frac{k}{k+1} + \frac{1}{(k+1)(k+2)}$$
$$= \frac{k(k+2)+1}{(k+1)(k+2)}$$
$$= \frac{(k+1)^2}{(k+1)(k+2)}$$
$$= \frac{k+1}{k+2}.$$

Hence, if the result is true for $n = k$, then it is true for $n = k+1$. Since it is true for $n = 1$, it is true for all positive integer values of n.

An alternative deductive proof of this result uses the fact that each term of the series can be written as the difference of two fractions:

$$\frac{1}{1.2} + \frac{1}{2.3} + \frac{1}{3.4} + \ldots + \frac{1}{n(n+1)} = \left(1 - \frac{1}{2}\right) + \left(\frac{1}{2} - \frac{1}{3}\right) + \ldots + \left(\frac{1}{n} - \frac{1}{n+1}\right)$$
$$= 1 + \left(-\frac{1}{2} + \frac{1}{2}\right) + \left(-\frac{1}{2} + \frac{1}{3}\right) + \ldots + \left(-\frac{1}{n} + \frac{1}{n}\right) - \frac{1}{n+1}$$
$$= 1 - \frac{1}{n+1}$$
$$= \frac{n}{n+1}.$$

Page 56, 4.5, Question 5

The result holds for $k = 1$, assuming the result that $\dfrac{d}{dx}(x^{-1}) = \dfrac{-1}{x^2} = -1x^{-2}$.

Suppose that it is true for $n = k$: $\dfrac{d}{dx}(x^{-k}) = -kx^{-k-1}$.

Then, using the product rule:

$$\frac{d}{dx}(x^{-k-1}) = \frac{d}{dx}(x^{-k}.x^{-1}) = x^{-1}.-kx^{-k-1} + x^{-k}.-x^{-2} = -(k+1)x^{-k-2}.$$

The right-hand expression has the same form as the original, but with $k+1$ in place of k. Thus, if the result is true for $n = k$ then it is true for $n = k+1$. Since it is true for $n = 1$, it is true for all positive integer values of n

Page 56, 4.5, Question 6

Since $2^3 > 2 \times 3$, the result is true for $n = 3$, but note that it is not true for $n = 2$.

If $2^k > 2k$, then multiplying both sides by 2 gives $2^{k+1} > 4k$.

Now $4k = 2k + 2k > 2k + 2 = 2(k+1)$ when $k > 1$, so $2^{k+1} > 2(k+1)$ when $k > 2$.

So, if the result is true for $n = k$, then it is true for $n = k+1$. Since it is true for $n = 3$, it is true for all $n > 2$.

Page 57, 4.6

The inductive step from $n = k$ to $n = k+1$ is valid when $k > 1$, but it breaks down in going from $n = 1$ to $n = 2$. You cannot deduce that any pair of people have the same height from the fact that any person has the same height as herself or himself.

If it were true that any pair of people have the same height, you could certainly say that any group of three would all be of the same height. So, you can go from 2 to 3 and similarly for higher values, but you cannot go from 1 to 2.

Page 58, 5.1

Each of the 12 isosceles triangles forming the regular dodecagon has a vertical angle of $30°$ and an area of $\frac{1}{2}r^2 \sin 30° = \frac{1}{4}r^2$ since $\sin 30° = \frac{1}{2}$.

Hence, the area of the regular dodecagon is $12 \times \frac{1}{4}r^2 = 3r^2$.

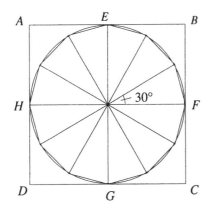 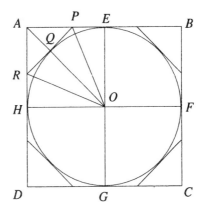

Each of the 8 isosceles triangles forming the regular octagon has a base whose length is equal to PR.

Now $PR = 2AQ$, since triangles AQP and AQR are congruent isosceles right-angled triangles. $AQ = AO - QO = r(\sqrt{2} - 1)$, so $PR = 2r(\sqrt{2} - 1)$.

The area of triangle OPR is $\frac{1}{2}PR \times QO = (\sqrt{2} - 1)r^2$.

Hence, the area of the regular octagon is $8(\sqrt{2} - 1)r^2$.

The dodecagon has a smaller area than the circle, so the area of the circle is greater than $3r^2$. The area of the circle is less than the area of the octagon which is $3.314r^2$ rounded to 3 decimal places. The area of the circle is, therefore, certainly less than $3.32r^2$.

> Note that there is a neat way of finding the area of a regular dodecagon in the Mathematical Association's book of readings *'Pig' and Other Tales* in the item about the fascinating dissection called Kürschak's Tile.

87

Page 59, 5.2

Let $S_1, S_2, S_3, \ldots$ be the areas of the bases of the solid sectors.

Volume of sphere $\approx \frac{1}{3}S_1r + \frac{1}{3}S_2r + \frac{1}{3}S_3r + \ldots = \frac{1}{3}r(S_1 + S_2 + S_3 + \ldots)$.

Now $S_1 + S_2 + S_3 + \ldots \to 4\pi r^2$, the surface area of the sphere, as the number of solid sectors is increased. Hence, volume of sphere $= \frac{1}{3}r.4\pi r^2 = \frac{4}{3}\pi r^3$.

Page 65, 5.3

$f(x) = x^2$

$$f'(x) = \lim_{h \to 0}\left(\frac{f(x+h) - f(x-h)}{2h}\right)$$

$$= \lim_{h \to 0}\left(\frac{(x+h)^2 - (x-h)^2}{2h}\right)$$

$$= \lim_{h \to 0}\left(\frac{4xh}{2h}\right)$$

$$= \lim_{h \to 0}(2x)$$

$$= 2x.$$

$f(x) = x^4$

$$f'(x) = \lim_{h \to 0}\left(\frac{f(x+h) - f(x-h)}{2h}\right)$$

$$= \lim_{h \to 0}\left(\frac{(x+h)^4 - (x-h)^4}{2h}\right)$$

$$= \lim_{h \to 0}\left(\frac{8x^3h + 8xh^3}{2h}\right)$$

$$= \lim_{h \to 0}\left(4x^3 + 4xh^2\right)$$

$$= 4x^3.$$

Note that the gradient of the chord in the case of $f(x) = x^2$ gives the exact value of the derivative regardless of the value of h. In other words, the chord is always parallel to the tangent at the point being considered.

$f(x) = \dfrac{1}{x}$ for $x \neq 0$

$$f'(x) = \lim_{h \to 0}\left(\frac{f(x+h) - f(x-h)}{2h}\right)$$

$$= \lim_{h \to 0}\left(\frac{\dfrac{1}{x+h} - \dfrac{1}{x-h}}{2h}\right)$$

$$= \lim_{h \to 0}\left(\frac{(x-h) - (x+h)}{2h(x^2 - h^2)}\right)$$

$$= \lim_{h \to 0}\left(\frac{-2h}{2h(x^2 - h^2)}\right)$$

$$= \lim_{h \to 0}\left(\frac{-1}{x^2 - h^2}\right)$$

$$= -\frac{1}{x^2}.$$

$f(x) = \cos x$

$$f'(x) = \lim_{h \to 0}\left(\frac{f(x+h) - f(x-h)}{2h}\right)$$

$$= \lim_{h \to 0}\left(\frac{\cos(x+h) - \cos(x-h)}{2h}\right)$$

$$= \lim_{h \to 0}\left(\frac{-2\sin x \sin h}{2h}\right)$$

$$= -\sin x \lim_{h \to 0}\left(\frac{\sin h}{h}\right)$$

$$= -\sin x.$$

Page 66, 6.1

You may be tempted to think that there are 32 regions with 6 points, but that is wrong. There are only 31 regions as a carefully drawn picture will make clear. So, unfortunately, the relationship between R and n is not a matter of powers of 2. The 'obvious' pattern is not always the right one! The correct result is revealed on page 67.

Page 67, 6.2

$R = 386$ when $n = 11$. Doubling gives 1024 for $n = 11$, which is clearly not plausible! With larger values of n the disparity is much greater: $n = 20$ gives $R = 5036$ whereas doubling would give 524288, which is more than 100 times greater.

Page 68, 6.3

It is impossible to draw the diagram as shown. If the point H lies on AC produced then G must lie between A and B, not on AB produced, leading to the incorrect statement that $AB = AG - BG$. Try drawing an accurate diagram for yourself! Nonetheless, a figure, however accurate, does not prove anything – there must be a reason why the points G and H must be as suggested above. Since $ABFC$ is a cyclic quadrilateral, one of the opposite angles at B and C must be greater than a right angle and the other less than a right angle.

Page 70, 6.4

Here are three false sums for this series:

a) $S = (1 - 2) + (4 - 8) + (16 - 32) + \ldots$

$\qquad = -1 - 4 - 16 - \ldots$

$\qquad \to -\infty.$

b) $S = 1 - (2 - 4) - (8 - 16) - (32 - 64) \ldots$

$\qquad = 1 + 2 + 8 + 32 + \ldots$

$\qquad \to \infty.$

c) $\qquad\qquad S = 1 - 2 + 4 - 8 + 16 - 32 + \ldots$

$\qquad$ Then, $2S = 2 - 4 + 8 - 16 + 32 - \ldots$

$\qquad$ Adding: $3S = 1 \implies S = \dfrac{1}{3}.$

The last result is equivalent to using the formula for the sum of a geometric series with a common ratio of $^-2$ which is not valid.

Bibliography and Further Reading

Allenby, RBJT	Numbers and Proofs Arnold, 1997, 0 340 67653 1
Baylis, J and Haggarty, R	Alice in Numberland Macmillan, 1988, 0 333 44242 3
Boyer, C and Merzbach, U	A History of Mathematics (2nd edition) Wiley, 1991, 0 471 54397 7
Cockcroft, WH	Mathematics Counts HMSO, 1982, 0 11 270522 7
Davis, PJ and Hersh, R	The Mathematical Experience Penguin Books, 1983, 0 14 022456 4
Euclid	The Elements, Books 1 and 2 Dover, 1956, 0 486 60088 2
French, DW and Stripp, C (editors)	'Pig' and Other Tales: A Book of Mathematical Readings Mathematical Association, 1997, 0 906 58838 3
Gardiner, A	The Mathematical Olympiad Handbook Oxford University Press, 1997, 0 19 850105 6
Hardy, GH	A Mathematician's Apology Cambridge University Press, 1992, 0 521 42706 1
Lakatos, I	Proofs and Refutations Cambridge University Press, 1976, 0 521 29038 4
Mason, John	Learning and Doing Mathematics Macmillan, 1988, 0 333 44942 8
Nelsen, RB	Proofs without Words Mathematical Association of America, 1993, 0 88385 700 6
Polya, George	How to Solve It Penguin Books, 1990, 0 14 012499 3
Price, M and Richardson, J	Exploring Mathematical Topics, Pack 1 Pearson Publishing, 1995, 1 85749 217 X
Singh, Simon	Fermat's Last Theorem Fourth Estate, 1997, 1 85702 521 0
Stewart, Ian	Nature's Numbers Weidenfeld & Nicolson, 1995, 0 297 81642 X
Vakil, Ravi	A Mathematical Mosaic: Patterns and Problem Solving Brendan Kelly, Ontario, 1996, 1 895 99704 6
Watson, FR (editor)	Proof in Mathematics ('if', 'then' and 'perhaps') University of Keele, 1978, No ISBN